PRAYING THE ROSARY
for Intercession

PRAYING THE ROSARY
for Intercession

Catherine M. Odell

Our Sunday Visitor Publishing Division
Our Sunday Visitor, Inc.
Huntington, Indiana 46750

Nihil Obstat
Msgr. Michael Heintz, Ph.D.
Censor Librorum

Imprimatur
✠ Kevin C. Rhoades
Bishop of Fort Wayne-South Bend
March 19, 2012

The *Nihil Obstat* and *Imprimatur* are official declarations that a book is free from doctrinal or moral error. It is not implied that those who have granted the *Nihil Obstat* and *Imprimatur* agree with the contents, opinions, or statements expressed.

ISBN: 978-1-59276-801-1 (Inventory No. T1106)
eISBN: 978-1-61278-216-4
LCCN: 2012933148

Cover design: Amanda Falk
Cover art: *The Nativity*, c.1490 (oil on panel) (detail of 201617)
by Lorenzo Costa (1459/60-1535), Musée des Beaux-Arts,
Lyon, France/Giraudon/The Bridgeman Art Library
Interior design: Sherri L. Hoffman

PRINTED IN THE UNITED STATES OF AMERICA

To all those
who pray, promote, and love the Rosary,
an enduring "lifeline" to the loving Mother of God

TABLE OF CONTENTS

INTRODUCTION

This book joins many other books about the Rosary. They are written in every language under the sun, and these works offer us the wisdom and experience of the saints, the teachings of the Church, and the testimony of countless prayerful brothers and sisters from the present and the past. These books hold up the Rosary, sometimes called "the Bible on a string," and encourage us to learn about it and pray with it — for ourselves and for the world.

Testimonies about the spiritual fruits and blessings that come from the Rosary have been stacking up for centuries. They come from popes, saints, Doctors of the Church, theologians, and ordinary Catholics and other Christians. They come from the visionaries of Marian apparitions, particularly the visionaries of Lourdes (1858) and the three visionaries of Fátima (1917).

The more modern complaint that the Rosary encouraged a rote and mindless repetition of Aves (Hail Marys) has certainly had its day. Almost every cradle Catholic has a story about an uncle or a parish priest (the stories are usually about men) who rattled off the Rosary in five minutes flat when it was being prayed aloud and in a group.

A falloff in the widespread popularity of the Rosary did occur after the Second Vatican Council. That was "an unintended outcome of the council's efforts to refocus Catholics on Jesus, sacred Scripture and the liturgy," wrote Dr. Thomas H. Groome, professor of theology and religious education at Boston College. Groome's perspectives were shared in "How the Rosary Teaches Us to Pray: My Mother Always Said, 'Just Think about the Mysteries' " (*Catholic Digest*, October 2005). Personally, Groome said that he learned rich lessons from the Rosary, which his family prayed every night. "It convinced me that we can go to Jesus through Mary, and that a great communion of saints prays with us. It taught me the responsibility of praying by myself as well as with others; it taught me that I could pray just about anytime and anyplace."

When the Rosary is carefully examined, it is easy to see the truth in the statement made by Pope Paul VI, who borrowed the insight from his predecessor, Pope Pius XII: "The Rosary is the compendium of the entire Gospel." The line was often quoted by Pope John Paul II (now also known as Blessed John Paul II), whose 2002 apostolic letter *Rosarium Virginis Mariae* ("The Rosary of the Virgin Mary") did more to rejuvenate the reputation and interest in the Rosary than anything else in the last several centuries.

Leaning on the worldwide devotion he rightfully garnered over his long and vibrant papacy, the pope admitted that he had been devoted to Mary and to the Rosary from his seminary days.

"The Rosary has accompanied me in moments of joy and in moments of difficulty," Pope John Paul II told the world in his apostolic letter. "To it I have entrusted any number of concerns; in it I have always found comfort. Twenty-four years ago, on 29 October 1978, scarcely two weeks after my election to the See of Peter, I frankly admitted: 'The Rosary is my favorite prayer. A marvelous prayer!' " (n. 2).

In May 2008, John Paul's successor, Pope Benedict XVI identified "a new springtime" for the Rosary. In his travels around the world, he said, he saw many young people praying the Rosary. "Without a doubt," the pope said, "this is one of the most eloquent signs of love that the young generation nourish for Jesus and his Mother, Mary."

HOW TO USE THIS BOOK

The Rosary, as a prayer of intercession, is the special focus of this book. It can be used in a variety of ways. Those who already know the Rosary might wish to read it cover to cover. That is a good way to renew an appreciation for the history of the prayer as well as the meaning of the Rosary's twenty mysteries that are rooted in Scripture.

Hopefully, the features that are provided for each mystery also offer something new. These features (which follow the Scripture passages and reflections) give witness to the power of the prayer to transform, renew, strengthen, and direct those who pray it faithfully and reflectively. They also show the many ways that the Rosary works as an intercessory prayer. In the spirit of the Communion of Saints, these testimonials about the Rosary share true stories from the lives of the beatified and the canonized as well as the stories of ordinary Catholics among us.

Many readers who have prayed the fifteen-mystery Rosary for many years may wish to spend extra time reading and reflecting on the chapters that present the Luminous Mysteries (Mysteries of Light). These new Rosary mysteries, most Rosary devotees agree, are a wonderful gift to the devotion and to those who pray. They bring a richer, fuller understanding of the public life of Jesus.

Newcomers to the Rosary will want to read and learn about the Rosary by making their way through the book in the normal fashion. At the same time, however, they can use the final chapter, "As You Pray: A Hands-on Guide to the Rosary," as a user-friendly manual. It offers step-by-step instructions for praying the Rosary as well as short mystery prayers and prayer prompts for intercessory prayer.

THE POWER AND PRACTICE
OF INTERCESSORY PRAYER

INTERCEDING IN PRAYER

Like many words used to describe human relationships, "intercede" has a rich and thought-provoking array of meanings:

- To plead on another's behalf.
- To attempt to reconcile differences between two or more people or groups.
- To act as mediator in a dispute.

Look again at these definitions.

Clearly, the person who intercedes and acts as an intercessor has a very active role. This is a person who is willing to become involved in a struggle — in fact, in someone else's struggle. This is a person who plans to persist until the goal is accomplished. This is a person who is willing to put the needs and concerns of another person or group first. The intercessor is also one who sees and understands different points of view or concerns.

That first definition, however, suggests that an intercessor's role can ask a great deal more. It can ask for our hearts. Sometimes, the person who intercedes must do so with great passion and deep commitment. This intercessor is not just advocating or representing someone as a defense attorney would. This intercessor is *pleading*, begging on behalf of another person in need.

INTERCEDING AS CHRISTIANS

Since the birth of the Church at Pentecost almost two thousand years ago, Christians have been asked to pray

for one another and for the world. This loving and gener-
ous prayer helps to sustain and strengthen the Church, the
Body of Christ. And when the living followers of Jesus ask
saints in heaven to support their prayers to our compassionate God, prayer reaches another dimension. We call this
community of Christians, living and dead, the Communion
of Saints. *Lumen Gentium* (Dogmatic Constitution on the
Church), one of the most important documents issued by
Vatican II, clearly states that the saints of heaven "do not
cease to intercede with the Father for us, showing forth the
merits which they won on earth through the one Mediator
between God and man [Jesus Christ]" (n. 49).

What a comfort this should be for us! What an amazing
and wonderful reality is this Communion (or Community)
of Saints! A saint martyred in one of the earliest Roman
persecutions prays for us. A Jesuit missionary who died
largely unknown in seventeenth-century North America
adds his voice, asking God to help us. Our great-great-
grandparents, whom we never knew, seek the Father's help
for us. Blessed Mother Teresa of Calcutta, Blessed John
Paul II, and perhaps a favorite teacher who has gone to God
could be interceding for us too.

Interceding for others in prayer and asking those in
heaven to add their prayers to ours is a powerful spiritual
tool. It is founded on the unity we share in Christ. The
living and the dead are the brothers and sisters of Christ
and the children of the Father. As Luke's Gospel tells us,
Jesus often talked about this Father's generosity and compassion:

> "And I tell you, ask and you will receive; seek and
> you will find; knock and the door will be opened to
> you. For everyone who asks, receives; and the one who
> seeks, finds; and to the one who knocks, the door will
> be opened. What father among you would hand his son

a snake when he asks for a fish? Or hand him a scorpion when he asks for an egg?" (Luke 11:9-12)

THE MEANING OF PRAYER

So, what is prayer? Though thousands of books have been written about it for many centuries, one of the most useful explanations of prayer is more than a thousand years old. Prayer is the "raising of one's heart and mind to God," wrote the eighth-century Doctor of the Church St. John Damascene. John's thoughtful and timeless interpretation of prayer has stood the test of time and has worn well in every Christian culture. The *Catechism of the Catholic Church* uses it at the beginning of its section on Christian prayer.

When one's heart and mind is raised to God on behalf of another, the *Catechism* explains, it is intercessory prayer. Intercessory prayer, the *Catechism* continues, is one of the five forms of prayer (CCC 2634-2636). Intercessory prayer is rooted in life-giving love. "The intercession of Christians recognizes no boundaries: 'for all men, for kings and all who are in high positions,' for persecutors, for the salvation of those who reject the Gospel" (CCC 2636).

INTERCESSION IN THE OLD TESTAMENT

Although the New Testament is bursting with examples of intercessory prayer — especially in the life and ministry of Jesus — it takes more careful looking to find them in the Old Testament. A shining example, Old Testament scholars tell us, is the story of Abraham's intercession on behalf of the sinful cities of Sodom and Gomorrah (Genesis 18-19). When Abraham hears that God plans to destroy the two cities, the patriarch begins to intercede, begging the Lord to spare Sodom and Gomorrah if enough innocent people can be found there.

In fact, Abraham bargains back and forth with God on behalf of these cities, which are nearby. Abraham asks for the Lord's mercy if fifty innocent residents can be found:

> "Will you really sweep away the righteous with the wicked? Suppose there were fifty righteous people in the city; would you really sweep away and not spare the place for the sake of the fifty righteous people within it?" (Genesis 18:23-24)

God agreed to spare the cities if there were fifty innocent people. Then, Abraham asked God to spare the cities if there were forty-five, forty, thirty, twenty, and then if only ten good or innocent people could be found in Sodom.

Time after time, God honored Abraham's prayerful request. Eventually, however, two angels sent by God looked for but did not find ten innocent people in the cities of Sodom and Gomorrah. Except for Lot and his family, all the inhabitants of Sodom and Gomorrah — and the cities themselves — were subsequently destroyed. (Scripture scholars suggest that an earthquake likely leveled the cities and that fires spontaneously erupted. In this region, combustible bitumen is commonly found in the soil.)

So, this remarkable Old Testament story shows us a God who is waiting and ready to forgive and respond. God is listening.

INTERCESSION IN THE NEW TESTAMENT

The four Gospels report that Jesus was constantly interceding in prayer for those who asked for his help. This included, of course, those seeking healing. Jesus also often prayed alone for others. In Luke 6:12, the evangelist writes, "In those days he departed to the mountain to pray, and he spent the night in prayer to God." On this particular occasion, Jesus must have been praying for those who would one day share the Gospel with the rest of the world. Luke continues to report that "when day came, he called his disciples to himself, and from them he chose Twelve, whom he also named apostles" (Luke 6:13).

One of the most dramatic occasions of Jesus interceding, however, appears in John 11 — the raising of Lazarus from the dead.

When Jesus finally arrives in Bethany near Jerusalem, he finds that Lazarus has already been dead and buried for four days. In the beautiful dialogue between Jesus and Martha and Mary, the sisters of the dead man, Jesus reminds them that he himself is the resurrection and the life. Faith in him assures life for the believer. The two women, close friends and avid students of his teaching — probably for years — understand. Jesus is promising that their only brother will have an eternal *spiritual* life.

But then, Jesus, in front of a crowd, asks that the stone in front of the tomb of Lazarus be rolled away. Speaking aloud, he thanks God for answering the prayer he has already prayed for the physical resurrection of Lazarus. Then Jesus calls loudly, "Lazarus, come out!"

In a few moments, as the mourners and villagers watch and wait breathlessly, a figure still wrapped in a white shroud stumbles out of the tomb and into the sunlight. The prayer of Jesus has been answered. Lazarus has been brought back to life after dying four days earlier.

In raising Lazarus, Jesus certainly interceded for Martha and Mary, who loved their brother dearly. But he was also pleading for Lazarus, who was still a fairly young man. According to John's Gospel, this astounding prayer and work of Jesus had much greater meaning. Jesus intended to prove that he was the Son of God and that he had been sent by the Father. "I know that you always hear me," Jesus announces. "But because of the crowd here I have said this, that they may believe that you sent me" (John 11:42).

The raising of Lazarus by Jesus was earthshaking on many levels. The chief priests and Pharisees knew it immediately and were terrified. Dozens — perhaps hundreds — of people saw a man who was dead for four days come back to life! This miracle and the identity of Jesus could not be denied. It seemed clear to members of the Sanhedrin that the Romans would crush the Jewish people in order to end any popular uprising on behalf of Jesus. From then on, the Jewish leaders plotted to kill both Jesus and Lazarus.

In the Acts of the Apostles, the new communities of those who followed Jesus were always praying for others. The apostles of Jesus continued to boldly share the Good News. Often, they prayed for the needs of others "in the name of Jesus" because Jesus came to heal, to free, and to redeem.

On one occasion, when Peter and John were entering the Temple in Jerusalem, they met a man crippled from birth who was begging for alms. The apostles told the beggar that they had no money but could give him something better than money. Then Peter said, "What I do have I give you; in the name of Jesus Christ the Nazorean, [rise and] walk" (Acts 3:6). Peter took the astonished man by his right hand and helped him stand — for the first time in his life!

As the Acts of the Apostles says, this unnamed man walked into the Temple with Peter and John. People inside the Temple recognized that he was the cripple who used to beg at the Beautiful Gate. Perhaps they had seen him there for years. The beggar praised God and pointed out Peter and John as the two who had interceded in prayer for his healing. Certainly this was a man who would never forget the power of prayer or God's sweet mercy.

INTERCESSION IN CHRISTIAN HISTORY

After the first Christian century, stories of intercessory prayer could be found everywhere among the followers of

Jesus. But the account of St. Monica (322-387) and her son St. Augustine of Hippo (d. 430) is surely one of the most inspirational in Christian history. Both were born in the fourth century in northern Africa — then a Roman province.

Monica, a devout Christian, was married to a rough and volatile Roman official, Patricius. Patricius was a pagan and initially had only scorn for his wife's religious practices, especially her practice of giving alms to the poor. Monica and Patricius had three children — a son, Augustine, a second son, Navigius, and a daughter, Perpetua. Monica was completely devoted to her children but worried most about her brilliant and oldest child, Augustine. As he later admitted in his autobiography, *Confessions*, he was lazy and rebellious. When he went away to school, Augustine began to live a worldly and immoral lifestyle. Monica was devastated when Augustine later admitted that he had been living with a young woman and had fathered a child, Adeodatus. Augustine also embraced heretical religious beliefs taught by Manichaeism.

There was nothing that Monica could do to save her son — except to pray for him. Monica did pray for Augustine for many, many years. Like many intelligent young people from privileged backgrounds, he ignored — and even showed contempt — for his Christian mother's prayers and concerns.

Year after year, Monica interceded in prayer for her wayward son. She even consulted the advice of a bishop who had once been a Manichaean himself. The bishop declined to intercede with the young and unruly Augustine. He told the desperate and tearful mother that it would do no good. Anyone could see that Augustine was not yet ready to change. But the bishop predicted that "the child of those tears shall never perish." In 387, the petitions of St. Monica were finally answered, as her thirty-three-year-old son was baptized by St. Ambrose in Milan.

Because of the stubborn, intercessory prayers of Monica, Augustine became one of the greatest saints and theologians of the Church. Augustine's mother became one of our greatest models for persistent, loving, intercessory prayer.

In Book 3 of *Confessions*, Augustine gave a grateful and heartfelt testimony to the persistent prayers of his mother. He thanked God for drawing him from the "profound darkness" and for

> My mother, your faithful one, weeping to You for me, more than mothers weep the bodily deaths of their children. For she, by that faith and spirit which she had from You, discerned the death wherein I lay, and You heard her, O Lord; You heard her, and despised not her tears, when streaming down, they watered the ground under her eyes in every place where she prayed. Yes, You heard her.

Closer to our own century is the example of St. Thérèse of Lisieux (1873-1897). St. Thérèse, also affectionately called "the Little Flower," was born in Alençon, in northern France. She was the youngest of five girls born to a pious couple, Zelie and Louis Martin. The Martins put their children and their faith at the center of their lives. Thérèse was drawn to God from early childhood and entered the Carmelite convent at Lisieux at the age of fifteen.

As contemplatives, the Carmelites dedicated their prayer for certain intentions. The convent at Lisieux prayed for the ministry of priests. Though Thérèse was initially surprised by this, thinking that their souls were already "pure as crystal," she changed her mind during a monthlong pilgrimage in Italy, which she made before she entered the convent. She saw that priests were like other men and "still subject to human weakness. I understood my vocation in Italy," she admitted later.

Tragically, this vocation to prayer fully embraced by Thérèse was terribly short. She died at Lisieux of tuberculosis at the age of twenty-four. Before her death, she wrote her autobiography, *The Story of a Soul*. The book soon caught the attention of the whole Church. The accessibility of her spirituality, which she called "the little way," and her fresh and inspiring vision of the Communion of Saints quickly made her one of the most popular saints of the twentieth century.

Thérèse had once dreamed of becoming a missionary to China. Instead, she interceded for missionaries with such conviction and fervor that, in 1927, the Church named her co-patron of the missions, with St. Francis Xavier. In 1997, Pope John Paul II declared the little Carmelite a Doctor of the Church. St. Thérèse of Lisieux, the contemplative who loved praying for others, became the thirty-third Doctor of the Church and the third woman in the history of the Church to be so honored.

Today, we have many uncanonized saints continuing the ministry of saints like Monica and Thérèse. There are those who, like Monica, intercede for their own children — or for someone else's children. There are those who pray for the dead, the sick, the poor, the unemployed, or nations at war. Many others intercede for grieving or depressed friends, for the end of war, or for the environmental healing of our planet. They are members of our families or members of our parish or faith communities. Intercessory prayer comes naturally to those who see clearly that they belong to the Body of Christ.

THE ROSARY'S HISTORY

How old is the Rosary? How did it come to be, that treasured circle of beads, which generations have used to plead for the intercession of Mary, the Virgin Mother of God?

The Rosary prayer practice — and the physical Rosary itself — developed primarily in the Christian nations of Europe. The Rosary's evolution took many centuries — perhaps fifteen hundred years. The roots of the Rosary, of course, are found in the impulse to pray to the Blessed Virgin. That desire to direct prayers to Mary, the Mother of the Savior, can be documented from the fourth Christian century. But an orientation toward Mary really began in the first Christian century. The first apostles and disciples of Jesus were deeply devoted to her, and they honored her role in salvation history.

The earliest recorded prayer to Mary dates from the second or third century and was found written on papyrus in Egypt. It verifies that even in the infancy of the Church, the followers of Jesus understood Mary's importance. It is a short, simple prayer asking for her intercession. She is, after all, the Mother of God. Who would be better able to ask God to help us than the woman who gave birth to his Son?

> We turn to you for protection, Holy Mother of God.
> Listen to our prayers and help us in our needs.
> Save us from every danger, Glorious and blessed Virgin.

Centuries later, the prayer became known as the *Sub Tuum*, a shortened version of the full Latin title for the prayer — *Sub Tuum Praesidium* ("Under Your Protection"). Appealing for Mary's intercession and asking for her protection were themes that were repeated later in the *Memorare*, one of the most popular Marian prayers in Church history:

> Remember, O most gracious Virgin Mary, that never was it known that anyone who fled to thy protection, implored thy help, or sought thine intercession, was left unaided.

> Inspired by this confidence, I fly unto thee, O Virgin of virgins, my Mother. To thee do I come, before thee I stand, sinful and sorrowful. O Mother of the Word Incarnate, despise not my petitions, but in thy mercy hear and answer me. Amen.

The *Memorare* was often but erroneously attributed to St. Bernard of Clairvaux (1090-1153), a Doctor of the Church. It was likely written much later. Its popularization throughout France can definitely be credited to another Bernard: Father Claude Bernard (1588-1641). This seventeenth-century priest reported that he had been healed of a deadly illness immediately after praying the *Memorare*. From then on, Father Bernard constantly promoted the prayer among the prisoners and death-row inmates to whom he ministered.

Throughout the Middle Ages, as individual prayers in praise of Mary appeared, the format that the Rosary would use was already developing. In monasteries, monks had developed the prayer practice of reciting the 150 psalms — or, sometimes, fifty of them at a time. Because the lay brothers in the monastic communities were typically illiterate, they began the practice of saying the Our Father (Pater Noster) fifty times.

The practice of repeating the Lord's Prayer apparently became widespread in Christendom throughout the eleventh and twelfth centuries. Hollowed out stones, beads, berries, or pieces of bone were threaded onto a string that was tied in a circle. This circle of beads developed to help the conscientious keep track of their Pater Nosters. The strings of prayer beads themselves came to be known as "Paternosters." All over Europe, craftsmen who fashioned these early Rosaries were called "paternosterers."

The development of the Hail Mary prayer was still in the future. Older Catholic legends say that the Blessed Mother appeared to St. Dominic (d. 1221), showed him a Rosary, and then asked him to promote it. But many historians dispute the story and the claim that Dominic gave the Rosary to us. Letters and documents written during his lifetime make no mention of the Rosary. Nonetheless, the praying of the Hail Mary prayer (from Luke 1:28 and 1:42) was spreading throughout Christian Europe during Dominic's life and beyond. Historians say that the "Holy Mary, Mother of God" part of the prayer wasn't added until the late-fifteenth century. During the course of that century, however, a German Carthusian — not a Dominican — worked tirelessly to merge the recitation of the Hail Mary with the Psalter format. (Every Psalter was a manual of devotional prayers including the Book of Psalms and often the liturgical calendar and the Litany of Saints.) This created a Marian Psalter. In addition, the Carthusian advocated that those who prayed this Psalter refer to a Gospel verse after each Hail Mary. Other variations on this Marian Psalter were also developed and popularized.

By 1520, Pope Leo X officially authorized the Rosary for the entire Church, and fifty-two years later, in 1572, St. Pius V decreed that prayer to the Blessed Virgin through the Rosary would be celebrated as the feast of Our Lady of the Rosary on October 7. The specific Rosary prayers and their sequence were also standardized during this pope's reign. Pius, a Dominican and a former professor of theology and philosophy, was happy that he was able to do whatever a pope could do for the Rosary. He died soon after announcing the Rosary feast.

Several years earlier, Pius had inspired the formation of the Holy League, a military alliance of Catholic countries united to protect Europe from being overrun by the Muslim Ottoman Turks. On October 7, 1571, while the naval Battle of Lepanto was being fought between the Turkish navy and the greatly outnumbered fleets of the Holy League, the pope conducted a Rosary procession in St. Peter's Square.

Thousands of Romans participated in the Rosary procession and prayed with the Holy Father for victory. Before the battle began, sailors on every Holy League ship recited the Rosary with the papal legate. The Holy League was victorious in a five-hour battle. From then on, the Rosary was securely established in Europe as a powerful prayer of intercession — not just for individuals but also for entire nations.

In the last several centuries, other popes, theologians, and Catholic writers have extolled the Rosary as a spiritually enriching and powerful prayer practice. Among theologians, however, St. Louis-Marie Grignion de Montfort (1673-1716), a French Dominican, was certainly the most influential. He laid the modern foundations for Mariology and Marian devotion, especially the Rosary. Theologians predict that he will one day be named a Doctor of the Church.

While studying at the Saint-Sulpice Seminary in Paris, de Montfort paid for some of his tuition by working as a librarian in the seminary library. Since Saint-Sulpice was a great center for the study of spirituality, the young man had the opportunity to read almost everything written about Mary, the Mother of God.

Soon after his ordination in 1700, de Montfort joined the Dominican order and soon began to preach about the Rosary. He also established Rosary confraternities. Though he was constantly traveling on a mission circuit, he also poured his growing devotion to the Mother of God into writing about her. De Montfort's three Marian books — *True Devotion to Mary*, *The Secret of Mary*, and *The Secret of the Rosary* — became, and have remained, Marian spiritual classics.

Centuries later, the legacy of de Montfort's Rosary devotion deeply touched five popes: Pope Leo XIII (1810-1903), St. Pius X (1835-1914), Pope Pius XII (1876-1958), Pope Paul VI (1897-1978), and Pope John Paul II (1920-2005). Pope Leo XIII wrote twelve encyclicals and five apostolic letters focused on the Rosary. This pope, appropriately called "the Rosary pope," was the first pope of the twentieth century. Deeply concerned about secularism, he believed that a re-Christianizing of the world would have to show how Mary had an invaluable role in the redemption of humanity. It was a theological concept straight from the heart and writings of de Montfort.

In 1974, Pope Paul VI, who had presided over most of the Second Vatican Council and had a deep devotion to Our Lady, published an apostolic letter, *Marialis Cultus* (for the right ordering and development of devotion to the Blessed Virgin Mary). Years earlier, during a General Audience (October 8, 1969), the Holy Father promoted an enthusiastic embrace of Marian devotions for the post-conciliar Church. Praying the Rosary while contemplating its mysteries, he said, "sets our gaze and our mind upon Christ, the scenes of his life and their theological meaning, and does this not only with Mary, but also in the same way as Mary, insofar as this is possible for us. There is no doubt that no one ever gave more thought to him (cf. Lk 2:19; 2:51; 8:21; 11:28), understood him more, loved him more, and lived more like him." The Rosary, Pope Paul also said, "is the compendium of the entire Gospel."

In 2002, Pope John Paul II dramatically reintroduced the ancient prayer to a new millennium. He issued an apostolic letter, *Rosarium Virginis Mariae* ("The Rosary of the Virgin Mary"), announcing a Year of the Rosary. The Rosary, he explained, "has all the *depth of the Gospel message in its entirety*" (n. 1, emphasis in original).

As a young seminarian, Pope John Paul read de Montfort over and over. Later, his episcopal motto, "*Totus Tuus*" ("Totally Yours"), expressed his personal consecration to Mary. It was drawn from de Montfort's suggestion that Mary was more perfectly conformed to Jesus than anyone else could be. Because of that orientation in her, it followed that the more someone was consecrated to Mary, the more that person would be perfectly consecrated to Jesus — through Mary.

John Paul II also proposed that a new set of mysteries be added to the Rosary's Joyful, Sorrowful, and Glorious mysteries. The pope said that the five Mysteries of Light (or Luminous Mysteries) filled in the Rosary's Gospel gap. He meant that in meditating on the Gospel mysteries, there was no Rosary connection to Jesus between the Fifth Joyful Mystery — the Finding of Jesus in the Temple — and the First Sorrowful Mystery — the Agony in the Garden. Now, the Rosary's Luminous Mysteries walk one through the public life and ministry of Jesus. The journey begins with the Baptism in the Jordan and concludes near the end of Christ's ministry and life at the Institution of the Eucharist.

John Paul apparently borrowed the Luminous Mysteries concept from a Maltese priest, Father George Preca (1880-1962), whom he beatified in 2002. (Pope Benedict XVI canonized him in 2007.) Beloved on the island of Malta, the priest was affectionately called "Dun Gorg" (in English, Father George) by the people he served faithfully. Father George founded the Society of Christian Doctrine, a society of lay catechists who contributed greatly to the evangelization of Malta. For so many contributions to the growth of the faith, he was called "the second Apostle of Malta." (St. Paul the Apostle was "the first Apostle of Malta.") St. George Preca first proposed the Mysteries of Light in 1957.

So the Rosary continues to evolve as a living prayer practice of the Church. It also continues to appeal to the Christian world in new formats. Many Internet websites now instruct newcomers on the Rosary. They can learn how to pray it or learn all about its history as a beloved intercessory prayer. Several sites offer a virtual Rosary download that allows the user to click on the image of each bead as the prayer is recited. The color of the bead changes at the click to help the user "count" Hail Marys. Some Rosary websites with blogs provide electronic bulletin boards for those who want to share testimonies about the blessings that this enduring prayer brings into their lives. Phone applications (apps) are also available for download so that those who carry smartphones can still have a Rosary — an electronic one — in a purse or pocket.

Different types of Rosaries are constantly being produced and shared. "Earth Prayer Beads," for instance, guide the one praying in intercession for God's protection of a planet that increasingly suffers from environmental challenges. Chaplets, wrist rosaries, and finger rosaries, with just ten beads, offer options to those who want to pray the Rosary just one decade at a time.

Long ago, those with the impulse to pray dropped counted pebbles, one by one, to the ground. Over the centuries, the Rosary developed as a prayer tool. It evolved in every way to answer the need we have to pray. Through the centuries, the Rosary continued to develop and reflect the growing understanding of the Church about Mary.

Simply put, the Rosary can help us. It is in our God-given nature to raise our hearts to God. As Christians, we want to follow in the footsteps of Jesus and his Blessed Mother. The Rosary, a circle of fifty-nine beads with a cross, helps us to pray and meditate on the mysteries of salvation. It helps us tell heaven all about our joys, sorrows, and needs.

1. THE JOYFUL MYSTERIES

————————— *First Joyful Mystery* —————————

THE ANNUNCIATION

Scripture Passage

LUKE 1:26-38

In the sixth month, the angel Gabriel was sent from God to a town of Galilee called Nazareth, to a virgin betrothed to a man named Joseph, of the house of David, and the virgin's name was Mary. And coming to her, he said, "Hail, favored one! The Lord is with you." But she was greatly troubled at what was said and pondered what sort of greeting this might be. Then the angel said to her, "Do not be afraid, Mary, for you have found favor with God. Behold, you will conceive in your womb and bear a son, and you shall name him Jesus. He will be great and will be called Son of the Most High, and the Lord God will give him the throne of David his father, and he will rule over the house of Jacob forever, and of his kingdom there will be no end." But Mary said to the angel, "How can this be, since I have no relations with a man?" And the angel said to her in reply, "The holy Spirit will come upon you, and the power of the Most High will overshadow you. Therefore the child to be born will be called holy, the Son of God. And behold, Elizabeth, your relative, has also conceived a son in her old age, and this is the sixth month for her who was called barren; for nothing will be impossible for God." Mary said, "Behold, I am the handmaid of the Lord. May it be done to me according to your word." Then the angel departed from her.

Reflection

In many Bibles, this wonderful passage from Luke about the Annunciation is headed with the words "Announcement of the Birth of Jesus." Clearly, the focus of the passage is on Jesus — not Mary. The Gospel story about the Annunciation appears only in the Gospel of Luke. Luke tells us that the angel Gabriel was sent to Mary in her hometown, Nazareth. Gabriel announced that God had chosen Mary to be the mother of his son, Jesus. But the announcement was really more of an invitation or a request. Mary was no more than fifteen or sixteen years old, and had been engaged to Joseph, a carpenter.

What a blessing it is for the followers of Jesus to also hear the story of Christ's conception and birth from his mother's point of view. Matthew tells about the visit of the "angel of the Lord," who appeared to Joseph in a dream. Mark and John begin their Gospels by focusing on John the Baptist and his ministry. But isn't Mary's story an exquisite testimony for us?

Mary may have been a simple Hebrew teenager, but when the angel told her that God was asking her to become the mother of his Son, she had questions too. "How can this be," the girl asked the angel, "since I have no relations with a man?" (Luke 1:34). The angel's answer was reassuring. This child would be miraculously conceived in her. Unlike any other human baby, there would be no earthly father for Mary's son. But out of Gabriel's answer, a thousand new questions must have been born in Mary's heart. Among them:

- How can I explain this child to my parents?
- What shall I say to Joseph, my betrothed?
- What will the villagers and synagogue leaders say about me?
- If this child is truly the Son of God, how can I be a worthy mother?
- How will the world receive my son?
- Will they know that Jesus is God's Son?

- Will Jesus become the mighty King of Israel?
- What will my son look like?
- Why has God chosen me?

Despite the questions that were surely swirling through her mind and heart, Mary said yes to God. She knew that she had a choice. She was not being *forced* to become the mother of a miraculously conceived child. She was being *asked* to do it. Mary searched her sinless heart and made her decision. She answered yes to God, even though she had no idea what that yes would mean for herself, her child, Joseph, her family, and even for the world.

"Behold, I am the handmaid of the Lord. May it be done to me according to your word," she answered. Gabriel then departed. Mary was instantly pregnant with a divine child, the Son of God.

For centuries, Mary's yes to God at the Annunciation has been called her "fiat." *Fiat* is a Latin word that means "Let it be done." In a column in *Liguorian* magazine (January 2008), Catholic writer Paige Byrne Shortal once wrote that she wished that she could give God "a classy yes" like Mary did with "Let it be done to me according to your word." Her own yeses, Shortal added, were often less than wholehearted, as in "Okay, if you say so." That fiat of Mary, she added, was "a yes to the Unknown. These are the only yeses that really count."

The Rosary in Our Lives

A "Yes" to Life

Every family creates its own Christmas traditions, and one tradition that Mary Walorski really enjoyed was taking her daughters Annie and Sarah to the mall to finish Christmas shopping right before Christmas. By that time, Christmas was really in the air. The girls were on vacation from school, and the Christmas decorating and baking were done. It was fun for the "Walorski women" to finish their shopping together.

On the Friday before Christmas in 1994, Mary and her girls were in the midst of their annual "right before Christmas" mall trip. After several hours, the girls rendezvoused with their mother. When Mary glanced at her watch, she realized that she had forgotten that it was Friday! Every Friday at 12:30 p.m., a group of local people gathered near the local abortion clinic to recite the Rosary for an end to abortion. Mary was active in that prayer ministry. When her kids had free time, they often joined her.

Mary was torn. She didn't really want to cut short the mall trip. The girls were having fun, finding bargains and getting "perfect" gifts for each other and their friends. Mary considered skipping her prayer time at the abortion clinic. It was the Friday before Christmas, after all. "Nobody would be going for an abortion today," she told herself. Nonetheless, an urge to go and pray kept nagging her. She finally gave in and told the girls that she thought she should go to the abortion clinic to pray. The girls graciously agreed to cut short the mall trip and go with her.

When they arrived, Mary saw that the usual, loyal prayer people had already assembled. It was a cold day, and there was a lot of snow. Bundled-up intercessors were getting ready to walk a route in front of the clinic while praying the Rosary aloud. Prayer was clearly needed on this cold Friday. There were plenty of cars in the abortion clinic's parking lot.

In the midst of a Hail Mary, a large black SUV with darkened windows pulled past the prayer line and into the clinic lot. Two people — a man and a woman — got out of the SUV and entered the clinic without even looking at the Rosary group.

Back and forth through the snowy lot, the group made its way, praying, but with sobered spirits now. Another child was about to die. Just days before Christmas, unborn babies were losing their lives inside. It was business as usual at the abortion clinic.

Just as the group was finishing the Rosary, the same two people came out of the clinic and got back into their black SUV. As the car was pulling away, the window rolled down on the passenger's side.

Mary remembers bracing herself. Often, nasty or negative comments were hurled at the prayer group by those entering or exiting the clinic. Instead, the SUV came almost to a dead stop right near her, and she found herself looking straight into the face of a woman whose eyes were peaceful.

Suddenly, the woman shouted at Mary, but her voice was full of joy and excitement. "I didn't do it! I didn't do it," she shrieked. "Stay here and pray so that others won't. . . ." Then, the dark tinted window went up, and the SUV sped off.

The prayer group stood still for a few moments as the woman's words sank in. The intercessors had been asking the Blessed Mother to protect unborn children. It was the same sinless Blessed Mother who had once said yes to God, even though she didn't really know what that yes would mean. This nameless woman of a nameless unborn child was also saying yes. It would be a difficult yes. She was joyful because she had been touched by the truth. Her unborn child was a gift, a treasure. Perhaps she sensed, as Mary surely had, that God would protect and guide her.

"Then I realized," an amazed Mary Walorski later told friends, "how small my faith was. Weren't we asking in prayer for an end to abortion? Our Lady took our small and imperfect prayers and moved the heart of that woman to choose life, to say yes to God for her baby."

Mystery Prayer

God, you chose to invite Mary, a teenage girl in Nazareth, to be the sinless mother of your son, Jesus. Your shining angel Gabriel appeared to her announcing your request. Every day, you send invitations to me, as well. Mary, the Mother of Jesus, please help me to see the Father's invitations in my life. Ask God to strengthen me so that I may joyfully say yes to him, just as you did. Amen.

Mystery Intentions
- Humility and openness to God's will in our lives.
- Respect and reverence for the unborn child.
- The conception and birth of healthy children for couples who want to be parents.
- Your own intention(s).

————— Second Joyful Mystery —————

THE VISITATION

Scripture Passage
LUKE 1:39-56

During those days Mary set out and traveled to the hill country in haste to a town of Judah, where she entered the house of Zechariah and greeted Elizabeth. When Elizabeth heard Mary's greeting, the infant leaped in her womb, and Elizabeth, filled with the holy Spirit, cried out in a loud voice and said, "Most blessed are you among women, and blessed is the fruit of your womb. And how does this happen to me, that the mother of my Lord should come to me? For at the moment the sound of your greeting reached my ears, the infant in my womb leaped for joy. Blessed are you who believed that what was spoken to you by the Lord would be fulfilled."
    And Mary said:

"My soul proclaims the greatness of the Lord;
    my spirit rejoices in God my savior.
For he has looked upon his handmaid's lowliness;
    behold, from now on will all ages call me blessed.

The Mighty One has done great things for me,
  and holy is his name.
His mercy is from age to age
  to those who fear him.
He has shown might with his arm
  dispersed the arrogant of mind and heart.
He has thrown down the rulers from their thrones
  but lifted up the lowly.
The hungry he has filled with good things;
  the rich he has sent away empty.
He has helped Israel his servant,
  remembering his mercy,
according to his promise to our fathers,
  to Abraham and to his descendants forever."

Mary remained with her about three months and then returned to her home.

Reflection

It is about one hundred miles from Nazareth, where Mary lived, to Ein Karem. Tradition suggests that Ein Karem was the home of Mary's cousin and kinswoman Elizabeth and Elizabeth's husband Zechariah. The village of Ein Karem is about five miles from Jerusalem.

Luke's Gospel makes it clear that when Mary heard of the miraculous pregnancy of the aging Elizabeth, she immediately traveled to see her. Today, we might wonder why. Mary's journey, clearly inspired by the Holy Spirit, would have been difficult. Newly pregnant, Mary likely rode a donkey for three days or more. She would have had traveling companions — perhaps men from the family, or perhaps even Joseph.

In Mary's decision, there was likely a desire to help Elizabeth in the final months of her pregnancy. In ancient cultures, it was women who oversaw the care of the household's garden — and perhaps a small vineyard. It was also the women who traveled to the village well to draw out water needed for cooking and washing. Though Elizabeth, the wife of a priest, would have had servants to help, Mary's presence as a member of the family would have brought comfort to Elizabeth. Luke's Gospel makes it clear that Mary returned to Nazareth after three months — probably right after John's birth.

Mary also knew that her own miraculous pregnancy and Elizabeth's astonishing "late in life" pregnancy were wonderfully and mysteriously connected. Gabriel had assured her of that. God had a plan for these two unborn children. It was a plan that would renew Israel and redeem all people. Nonetheless, this teenage mother could only guess what events would eventually unfold through her son, Jesus, and the child Elizabeth was carrying. What she did know was that this mysterious future was in God's hands.

Luke suggests that Mary's heart simply overflowed with love and gratitude in a prayer we call the Magnificat. In fact, the prayer, also known as the Canticle of Mary, may have been a Jewish-Christian hymn that Luke included in the Gospel to show us the joyful heart of Mary. The word *magnificat* is the Latin word for "magnifies," the first word of the prayer in Latin. Mary could not remain silent about "the greatness of the Lord."

Inside the pure and selfless heart of this young girl, however, there was probably another reason for the visit. It was a very human, very endearing motive. Filled with the Holy Spirit, who is love, Mary saw that love is best communicated when we are present to the ones we love. Mary gave the very human gift of presence to Elizabeth.

In today's world of electronically transmitted sound and image, we often forget how important and powerful it is to be personally present to someone. We still crave that personal connection, the handshake, the hug, the eye-to-eye and face-to-face encounter.

Mary, the young girl from Nazareth, understood that ageless truth. We are made for community. We are happiest when we live with and for one another.

The Rosary in Our Lives

MARY, THE "FIRST" MISSIONARY OF CHARITY

On September 10, 1946, a petite, lively nun of Albanian heritage was on a train making its bumpy way from Calcutta to Darjeeling, India. Along with several other sisters, thirty-six-year-old Sister Mary Teresa was happy to be getting out of Calcutta. The city's oppressive, sticky heat, heavy with smells of all sorts, was exhausting. Each year, the sisters traveled north to make a retreat, spending quiet time in prayer. For many years, Sister Mary Teresa had been a popular and highly respected teacher at St. Mary's School for Girls in Calcutta. The little nun had joined the Sisters of Loreto, an Irish congregation, when she was about the age of the wealthy Indian girls she was then teaching.

Sister Teresa was looking forward to her quiet time with God. But God did not wait until Sister Teresa — the future Mother Teresa of Calcutta — reached the retreat house in Darjeeling. In a way that she was never willing to fully describe, Sister Teresa encountered Jesus on that trip. He told her of his pain over the neglect of the poor and their ignorance of him. In the weeks and months following, further visions and locutions clarified what Jesus wanted of her.

Mother Teresa later called this experience her "call within a call." She received a second vocation to the poorest of the poor following her initial vocation to religious life. On August 17, 1948, dressed in a simple white, blue-bordered sari, she left the Sisters of Loreto. She had been given permission to found a new order, the Missionaries of Charity.

Many years later, Mother Teresa of Calcutta, told Father Patrick Peyton, C.S.C., the founder of the Family

Rosary Crusade, that her international order of nuns was devoted to Eucharistic Adoration and the daily recitation of the Rosary.

The Rosary was very important to her and to her sisters, Mother Teresa said. She explained that her sisters used the Rosary "to proclaim the presence of the Good News — that God loves the world, that he loves each one of us." The sisters also tried to share Mary with those they ministered to, who were primarily Hindu. "It's so beautiful to see what she is doing in their lives," Mother Teresa told Father Peyton.

What's more, she told the "Rosary priest," she and her sisters had a special devotion to the Rosary's Visitation mystery.

When she reflected on the meaning of the Blessed Mother's visit to Elizabeth, Mother Teresa said, she saw that Our Lady was the "first Missionary of Charity." The Missionaries of Charity saw Mary this way "because she was the first one to carry Jesus as the handmaid of the Lord. The moment Jesus came into her life, she immediately went in haste to give Him to others. That going [to others with Jesus] is part of what we, as Missionaries of Charity should be and should do."

Indeed, that carrying of Jesus to others had taken the Missionaries of Charity to 123 countries by 1997, the year Mother Teresa died. The order had established more than 600 foundations as orphanages, homes for the dying, soup kitchens, hospices, and leprosy clinics.

Ten years after her death, the Missionaries of Charity included 5,000 nuns and 450 brothers worldwide. In 2003, Pope John Paul II beatified Mother Teresa of Calcutta.

Mystery Prayer

God, our Creator, you fashioned the loving heart of Mary, who became the mother of Jesus. In her joy over this great blessing, she traveled to see and assist her cousin Elizabeth. Mary gave the loving gift of her presence, her care, and her desire to help when help was needed. Mary, help me to lovingly share my presence and my help wherever I go. Amen.

Mystery Intentions
- Visiting and personal outreach to others.
- Ministry to pregnant mothers.
- Offering companionship, the gift of presence.
- Your own intention(s).

_____ *Third Joyful Mystery* _____

THE BIRTH OF OUR LORD

Scripture Passage
Luke 2:1-20

In those days a decree went out from Caesar Augustus that the whole world should be enrolled. This was the first enrollment, when Quirinius was governor of Syria. So all went to be enrolled, each to his own town. And Joseph too went up from Galilee from the town of Nazareth to Judea, to the city of David that is called Bethlehem, because he was of the house and family of David, to be enrolled with Mary, his betrothed, who was with child. While they were there, the time came for her to have her child, and she gave birth to her firstborn son. She wrapped him in swaddling clothes and laid him in a manger, because there was no room for them in the inn.

Now there were shepherds in that region living in the fields and keeping the night watch over their flock. The angel of the Lord appeared to them and the glory of the Lord shone around them, and they were struck with great fear. The angel said to them, "Do not be afraid; for behold, I proclaim to you good news of great joy that will be for all the people. For today in the city of David a savior has been born for you who is Messiah and Lord. And this will be a sign for you: you will find an infant wrapped in swaddling clothes and lying in a manger." And suddenly there was a multitude of the heavenly host with the angel, praising God and saying:

> "Glory to God in the highest
>   and on earth peace to those on whom his favor rests."

When the angels went away from them to heaven, the shepherds said to one another, "Let us go, then, to Bethlehem to see this thing that has taken place, which the Lord has made known to us." So they went in haste and found Mary and Joseph, and the infant lying in the manger. When they saw this, they made known the message that had been told them about this child. All who heard it were amazed by what had been told them by the shepherds. And Mary kept all these things, reflecting on them in her heart. Then the shepherds returned, glorifying and praising God for all they had heard and seen, just as it had been told to them.

Reflection

For thousands of years, the wonderful ironies of the Savior's birth in Bethlehem have fascinated the world. There are so many surprises! The Lord of the Universe was born in a drafty stable. His first visitors were definitely not movers and shakers of Israel who had rushed from Jerusalem for his arrival. They were rough, dirty, illiterate shepherds. The parents of this long-heralded "Messiah and Lord" were poor people from a sleepy backwater village named Nazareth.

It's true that the birth of the Messiah in Bethlehem was prophesied long before Jesus was born. The prophet Micah (5:1) had predicted it. But in so many worldly ways, the birth of Jesus Christ, the Redeemer, came with so many surprises. Shouldn't Christ have come into the world in a way that would have guaranteed the world's attention? Why wasn't the new king born comfortably in a palace? Advisers, historians, Jewish leaders, and many others could have been nearby to protect and welcome him. Today, media executives might be tempted to say that this world-changing "event" — the birth of Jesus Christ — was poorly promoted.

The answer is that God, our Father, is a God of surprises. He reminds us that "my thoughts are not your thoughts, / nor are your ways my ways" (Isaiah 55:8). He knows that the creatures he made in his own image also love surprises. As children, we are captivated by them and never really outgrow that trait.

Father Edward Schillebeeckx, the Flemish Dominican theologian who died at age ninety-five right before Christmas (December 23) in 2009, was once asked about his first conscious musings on Jesus. The white-haired scholar, who had written and taught so beautifully about Jesus, took only a moment to respond.

"The baby is God," he said.

That was what the theologian's father had told him one Christmas, when Edward was a very small child. The father had made the statement as he pointed, directing his little boy's attention to the infant Jesus in the large Christmas crib in their home. The wondrous miracle contained in his father's simple, matter-of-fact statement — stayed with Father Schillebeeckx throughout his long life. Perhaps this surprise — that God would come to earth as a baby — shaped him.

As a theologian, Father Edward Schillebeeckx contributed greatly to the renewal of Catholic sacramental theology and attended the Second Vatican Council. He defended and promoted the dramatic — and surprising — re-envisioning of the Church that was the fruit of Vatican II. He was also the first Catholic scholar to make use of modern historical research done on Jesus. He incorporated it into the accessible portraits of a loving, compassionate Jesus that he presented in his writings.

"Jesus was a surprise, the likes of whom no one expected," wrote fellow theologian Cardinal Joseph Ratzinger, who became Pope Benedict XVI. He shared the fascination

about Jesus that preoccupied Father Schillebeeckx throughout his long life. We have a Savior, the King of kings, who
was born in a stable.

The Rosary in Our Lives
MIRACLE AT BELLEVUE

Dorothy Day (1897-1980) had never given much thought
to Mary, the Mother of God, until the last months of the
winter of 1926. Her parents had been married in an Episcopal church, but Dorothy had drifted away from any active involvement in religion. When she lived and worked in
Chicago, she had accompanied Catholic friends to Mass.
She was attracted to Catholic liturgy and spiritual disci-
pline. By her mid-twenties, she had become an agnostic
and worked as a journalist in New York City for socialist
publications — *The Liberator*, *The Masses*, and *The Call*.

Everything was changing, however, as the twenty-eight-
year-old joyfully prepared to give birth to her first child.
She thought often about the pregnant Mary making that
difficult journey to Bethlehem. Mary would have been anxious, exhausted, and uncomfortable. She would also have
been so filled with life, joy, and gratitude to God. That's
what Dorothy felt too during the final few months of her
pregnancy. The world would be brand new with the birth
of her baby. A new human child, a unique human being,
would fill its lungs for the first time, with the wonderful
possibilities life offers.

By then, Day knew that the child's father, her common-
law husband, Forster Batterham, would soon leave her.
Batterham, an avowed anarchist, didn't believe in God,
marriage, or government. He was frustrated with her and
couldn't see any reason to bring new life into such a brutal,
chaotic world.

"But how can there be no God?" Dorothy argued with
Forster. All around her, she now saw the awesome handi-

work of a loving Creator. Dorothy believed that her pregnancy was God's message to her. Following the abortion of a child some years earlier, she had been told that she would not be able to conceive again. Now, at age twenty-eight, she wanted to live the rest of her life in a totally different way. She wanted to be part of the Catholic family, and she wanted that faith family for her child.

Dorothy began taking instructions so that her child could be baptized in the Catholic Church. "I began to think, to weigh things," she later said, "and it was at this moment that I began consciously to pray more." A friend gave her a statue of Mary, which she would treasure. She began to pray and also to read Scripture and Catholic theology. She adopted a lifelong habit of carrying a rosary and later prayed it every day after attending Mass.

Dorothy's daughter, Tamar Day Batterham, was born on March 3, 1927. Bellevue Hospital in New York City was not Bethlehem. But for Dorothy, there was a multitude of angels rejoicing over this new baby's birth. She raved about Tamar's "amazing blue eyes," her auburn hair, golden eyebrows, and beautiful tan complexion. On December 28, 1927, months after she had Tamar baptized, Dorothy herself was received into the Church. From then on, she was a deeply devoted Catholic.

By the time Tamar was five, her mother was more and more preoccupied with activism on behalf of the poor. In 1933, she co-founded *The Catholic Worker* newspaper with Peter Maurin. Soon after that, because millions of Americans were out of work, Catholic Worker houses of hospitality opened all over the country. Little Tamar was raised in Catholic Worker communities, as her mother traveled frequently.

For her child and for the needs of the poor, Dorothy Day clung to her rosary. She prayed it, she later wrote, "on the picket lines, in prisons, in sickness and in health." She turned to the Blessed Mother over and over in prayer. As a single mother, Dorothy constantly begged the Mother of God to help her with Tamar. She had grown to trust more and more in the Blessed Mother as a mother. Many Rosaries had taught her that. In fact, as Dorothy Day later told Catholic Worker friends: "I've turned Tamar over to the Blessed Mother."

Mystery Prayer

Father of the Redeemer, your angels filled the Bethlehem sky with rejoicing on the night your son, Jesus, was born. You gave the world the gift you had always promised. The Son of God was born among us. He came to live with us, to die for us, and to save us. Mary, you and Joseph welcomed the newborn Jesus with so much love. Help me to welcome Jesus into my heart and into my life each day. Amen.

Mystery Intentions
- Welcoming and caring for each child born.
- Protection and respect for children's rights.
- Support for families.
- Your own intention(s).

————— Fourth Joyful Mystery —————

THE PRESENTATION IN THE TEMPLE

Scripture Passage

Luke 2:22-40

When the days were completed for their purification according to the law of Moses, they took him up to Jerusalem to present him to the Lord, just as it is written in the law of the Lord, "Every male that opens the womb shall be consecrated to the Lord," and to offer the sacrifice of "a pair of turtledoves or two young pigeons," in accordance with the dictate in the law of the Lord.

Now there was a man in Jerusalem whose name was Simeon. This man was righteous and devout, awaiting the consolation of Israel, and the holy Spirit was upon him. It had been revealed to him by the holy Spirit that he should not see death before he had seen the Messiah of the Lord. He came in the Spirit into the temple; and when the parents brought in the child Jesus to perform the custom of the law in regard to him, he took him into his arms and blessed God, saying:

> "Now, Master, you may let your servant go in peace, according to
>   your word,
> for my eyes have seen your salvation,
>   which you prepared in sight of all the peoples,
> a light for revelation to the Gentiles, and glory for your people
>   Israel."

The child's father and mother were amazed at what was said about him; and Simeon blessed them and said to Mary his mother, "Behold, this child is destined for the fall and rise of many in Israel, and to be a sign that will be contradicted (and you yourself a sword will pierce) so that the thoughts of many hearts may be revealed." There was also a prophetess, Anna, the daughter of Phanuel, of the tribe of Asher. She was advanced in years, having lived seven years with her husband after her marriage, and then as a widow until she was eighty-four. She never left the temple, but worshiped night and day with fasting and prayer. And coming forward at that very time, she gave thanks to God and spoke about the child to all who were awaiting the redemption of Jerusalem.

When they had fulfilled all the prescriptions of the law of the Lord, they returned to Galilee, to their own town of Nazareth. The child grew and became strong, filled with wisdom; and the favor of God was upon him.

Reflection

In the first several centuries of Christianity, the earliest followers of Jesus celebrated his presentation in the Temple with great processions and joyful singing. This feast was celebrated exactly forty days after the celebration of the birth of Jesus. Since Christmas was eventually celebrated on December 25 in the Latin (Western) Church, the Presentation of the Lord was celebrated each year on February 2. As Luke's Gospel indicated, this feast had its roots in Mosaic law.

Jewish parents waited for forty days before taking a son to the Temple to be dedicated or presented. Mosaic law taught that a woman was ritually "unclean" for forty days after giving birth to a son, and for eighty days after giving birth to a daughter. An "unclean" woman could not participate in worship at the Temple until forty days had elapsed. Forty days after the birth of Jesus, Mary and Joseph made their way to the Temple for the baby's presentation and for Mary's purification.

Since Jesus was the firstborn child of Mary, Joseph and Mary also observed another Jewish law — the "Redemption of the Firstborn." The Jewish community never forgot that, in the Book of Exodus (13:2), the firstborn male of both human beings and animals was seen as "sacred." It was a particularly precious gift from the Creator, the giver of all life. Understanding and honoring this ancient tradition followed for centuries by the Jewish community, the parents of a firstborn baby boy customarily paid five shekels to "buy back" their child from God. The payment was made at the Temple in Jerusalem.

But why did Mary and Joseph do this? Why would they go to such efforts to observe Mosaic law and tradition? Surely they knew that they didn't need to "buy back" Mary's child from God. Jesus was the Son of God! And surely they recognized that giving birth to a child conceived through the mysterious power of the Holy Spirit had not really made Mary "unclean."

Probably, Mary and Joseph just wished to be faithful and obedient Jews. Their humble trust in their heritage and in the ancient law gave God room to unfold his plan.

What's more, their spirit of faithful and patient obedience was echoed in the wonderful story of Simeon and Anna, the other "major characters" in this Presentation story.

Simeon was neither a priest nor a Temple official. He and Anna were among the "pious Jews." These were Jews who were waiting for the so-called "consolation of Israel," the Messiah. Simeon had been told by the Holy Spirit that he would not die before seeing this Savior. At eighty-four, Anna had never stopped worshiping God with prayer and fasting. Even though both Simeon and Anna were very old, they had remained faithful, obedient, and patient. The wonderful light of their faith never dimmed.

This bright but patient light of faith has been associated with the feast of the Presentation since the beginning of the eighth century. At the end of the seventh century, Pope Sergius I added a candlelight procession to the celebration of the feast. Several centuries later, the act of blessing and distributing pure beeswax candles was added to the Presentation observance. As a result, the feast was then often called "Candlemas."

Blessed candles were to be used prayerfully throughout the year, inside and outside of the church. The candles — and the light they would give — symbolized Simeon's words to Mary and Joseph in Luke 2:32. Jesus would be "a light for revelation to the Gentiles, / and glory for your people Israel." Those lighted candles remind Christians that Jesus Christ himself identified with the light. "I am the light of the world," he said. "Whoever follows me will not walk in darkness, but will have the light of life" (John 8:12).

The Rosary in Our Lives

A LIGHT IN THE DARKNESS

When John Abdo and his wife decided to join twenty-eight other people from California on a pilgrimage to

Medjugorje in March 2005, he may have had a few more butterflies in his stomach about the trip than the others did.

John, then in his mid-forties, did have a certain devotion to the Rosary, and he always had one in his pocket — without fail! John knew very well that his mother had prayed the Rosary each day for her children. He also knew that many people believed that the Blessed Virgin Mary had been appearing each day at Medjugorje since 1981. Called the Queen of Peace, she was asking the world to turn back to God through fasting, reconciliation, and prayer.

The priest directing the pilgrimage asked the people going to Medjugorje to prepare themselves spiritually. He asked them to receive the sacrament of Reconciliation before they left. For his own reasons, John decided not to. It had been so many years since he had gone to confession. There were so many sins, horrible sins, to confess.

One night in Medjugorje, John's group gathered with pilgrims from around the world in St. James Church. After a talk by a local priest, everyone lined up to receive individual blessings from another priest who had an unusual spiritual gift. He could "read" hearts. When John reached the priest, he didn't have any particular prayer intention in mind. "Just a blessing, Father. That's all. I would just like God to bless me," John responded, when queried by the priest.

When the priest laid hands on John's head, however, he pulled his hands back immediately in shock. He bluntly told John that he would have to go to confession before his sinful soul could benefit from God's blessing. Shaking a bit, John did as he was told. He moved out of the blessing line and headed over to another part of the church where priests were hearing confessions. For the first time in over thirty years, John Abdo received absolution for his many sins. After his confession, he doubled back to the priest in the blessing line. He wanted to know if the priest really had been able to "read" his heart and soul — or was just following a hunch.

All through his youth and into his twenties, John Abdo had moved with a bad crowd. The father of his best buddy had been the head of the Mafia in his hometown, and John got into violent crime. He abused drugs and became a thief. But John had been good at getting away with the evil things he did. He was a master at deception.

The priest could "see" all of this — and more. He quickly whispered to John the names of the stores he had robbed, the women he had hurt, and the places where he had gotten into brawls. But then the priest looked John straight in the eye.

"Do you want to know why God allowed you to survive those violent years?" the priest confronted him. "It's because your mother dedicated you to God through her prayers. She was faithful and obedient to God. But she decided that she would pray an extra Rosary every day of her life so that you might be saved."

In his heart, John knew that the priest was telling him the truth. He had been shot, stabbed, and severely beaten. With shame, he recalled the night, many years earlier, when he had come home late to find the light on in his mother's bedroom. She was on her knees praying the Rosary. He had shaken his head in disbelief, shouting, "When are you going to stop this nonsense?"

After Medjugorje and his return home, John began to pray the Rosary with great joy and peace. He had almost forgotten what those feelings were like. Formerly an insomniac, he began to sleep soundly every night.

"This is not really my story," John said. "It's my mother's story, the story of a mother praying for her children." It's also a story, he said, that tells how light can conquer the darkness.

Mystery Prayer

Loving God, Mary and Joseph honored you and Jewish law. They presented Jesus at the Temple forty days after his birth, even though he was already consecrated to you. Their hearts were humble, faithful, and obedient. Mary, because you and Joseph were faithful, God answered the prayers of Simeon and Anna to see the Messiah. Help me to be faithful and strong, honoring what's expected of me, as I grapple with the demands of life. Amen.

Mystery Intentions

- Dedication of our children to God.
- Honoring religious customs and laws.
- Faithfulness in responsibilities.
- Your own intention(s).

Fifth Joyful Mystery

THE FINDING OF JESUS IN THE TEMPLE

Scripture Passage

LUKE 2:41-52

Each year his parents went to Jerusalem for the feast of Passover, and when he was twelve years old, they went up according to festival custom. After they had completed its days, as they were returning, the boy Jesus remained behind in Jerusalem, but his parents did not know it. Thinking that he was in the caravan, they journeyed for a day and looked for him among their relatives and acquaintances, but not finding him, they returned to Jerusalem to look for him. After three days they found him in the temple, sitting in the midst of the teachers, listening to them and asking them questions, and all who heard him were astounded at his understanding and his answers. When his parents saw him, they were astonished, and his mother said to him, "Son, why have you done this to us? Your father and I have been looking for you with great anxiety." And he said to them, "Why were you looking for me? Did you not know that I must be in my Father's house?" But they did not understand what he said to them. He went down with them and came to Nazareth, and was obedient to them; and his mother kept all these things in her heart. And Jesus advanced [in] wisdom and age and favor before God and man.

Reflection

Sometime in the past, almost all of us have had the terrifying experience of being lost. Perhaps it was only five panic-filled minutes as a child in a crowded department store. Maybe it was hours of lonely agony in the woods, where you were without a map, a cell phone, and a decent sense of direction.

In this Gospel reading from Luke, the panic over a lost child is only in the hearts of Mary and Joseph, but it was very real. Jesus, a twelve-year-old, likely never saw himself as "lost." According to commentators on Jewish law and history, at the age of twelve Jesus was now a "son of the law," an adult Jewish male. Probably, this was the reason that neither Mary nor Joseph immediately missed Jesus as their caravan left Jerusalem after the Passover. Mary knew that Jesus was no longer a child, required to travel with the women and children. Joseph recognized that Jesus had only recently become a "man." Joseph may have presumed that Jesus was more comfortable journeying back to Nazareth as he had through childhood.

What gut-wrenching fear Mary and Joseph must have felt when they discovered that Jesus was not in the caravan at all. Though Mary trusted in the Providence of God, she did not know what God had planned for Jesus. Mary and Joseph had been protecting this special child for twelve years. Was he in danger again?

After three harrowing days, Mary and Joseph finally spotted their boy. He was discussing theological questions with the Jewish teachers of the Temple. As Luke's Gospel explains, Mary confronted her son, taking him to task for causing them so much anxiety and pain. The boy countered, saying that he had work to do "in his Father's house."

This scene of Mary and Joseph with the pre-adolescent Jesus is one that some parents have fun discussing today. Was the young Jesus offering a first-century equivalent of a "smart remark"? Jesus did not apologize. However, he may have suddenly appreciated what his mother and foster-father had suffered. The crisis ended gracefully. "He went down with them and came to Nazareth, and was obedient to them."

The Rosary in Our Lives

SOMEWHERE IN UKRAINE

In 1994, Denis and Cathy Nolan agreed to let their teenage son, Colin, travel from Indiana to a small town in rural Russia near Moscow. Colin was to serve for the summer with a new community named *Pro Deo et Fratribus* ("For God and the Brethren"), which had an outreach to the poor there. The organization was guided by Bishop Pavel Maria Hnilica, S.J., of the former Czechoslovakia, who had helped to evangelize for the Church in Eastern Europe. Though only sixteen at the time, Colin had grown a great deal spiritually at Medjugorje, which the Nolan family had visited many times as devoted pilgrims. Denis and Cathy had also met and gotten to know Bishop Hnilica, who shared their enthusiasm for promoting Medjugorje and the messages of Our Lady of Peace.

Though the Nolans heard very little from Colin during his travels, they were grateful for the opportunity he had to serve the Church at such a young age. One night in August, however, when Colin was due to travel home, Cathy woke up at 3 a.m. She sensed that Colin was in some kind of danger, somewhere in Eastern Europe. Colin was one of eight Nolan children, and Cathy's motherly instincts had become finely honed over the years. More importantly, she and Denis were extremely devoted to prayer and had learned many years earlier about the tremendous prayer power of the Rosary. Cathy shook Denis awake and whispered, "We've got to pray for Colin. Something's wrong!"

Denis and Cathy got up. They went downstairs to a large prayer room they had added on to their house and began to pray. The Nolans prayed Rosary after Rosary for Colin's life and safety. They also prayed for their own peace of heart. They tried to fight off the anxious dread that worried parents suffer whenever a child seems to be missing or in danger. Cell phones were not yet widely available. There was no way to call or contact Colin.

About three days later, the Nolans had a call from Colin — from Moscow. Cathy's middle-of-the-night fears had been warranted. Colin had needed all the Rosary prayers that Denis and Cathy offered.

Colin had been traveling alone on a train rattling its way from Moscow through Ukraine. He was headed for Vienna, where he was to get a flight home. When the train was stopped at the border between Ukraine and Russia, foreigners were ordered off the train by border guards. The guards checked the passengers, one by one, making sure that they had the appropriate visas to travel through Ukraine.

On the long trip from Moscow to Vienna, Colin had been sleeping to pass the time. When he jumped up, awakened from a deep sleep, he left his wallet and money behind on the seat. Because his visa had not been stamped properly in Moscow, he looked suspicious to the guards. Unfortunately, the border guards had no sympathy for the skinny American boy who kept pointing to the train, babbling the few words of Russian he had picked up. To his horror, the rest of the passengers soon reboarded, and the train pulled out of the station. He was stuck at the border between two countries.

All alone, Colin had no money, no visa, no food, and no idea what to do. The guards would not let him make a phone call. He was utterly alone. He remembered his Rosary, shoved down in his jeans pocket, and reached for it. Cold, hungry, and increasingly frightened, Colin sat and slept on the bench in the train station at the border for two days and two nights. He prayed for help, having no idea that his parents were praying for help at the same time.

Finally, as Colin later told his parents, some Pakistani travelers — Hindus — saw him when they got off the train for the border passport check. One of them asked in English, "Why are you sitting here?" A dejected Colin explained that the guards wouldn't let him back on the train. He said that he had left his wallet on the train seat and that his visa papers were not stamped properly, so he couldn't proceed to Vienna and couldn't go back to Moscow.

The Pakistani businessman was moved with compassion for Colin. He got him a train ticket back to Moscow and quietly slipped money to the guards to let Colin get back on the train. Back in Moscow, Colin reconnected with Pro Deo et Fratribus, the community he had lived and served with. After his trauma, a plane ticket was quickly purchased for him. This time, Colin was to fly to Vienna and then back to the United States. Soon, Colin Nolan was on his way back to his parents, who had prayed to find him. Colin and his parents believe it was the Rosary that protected him, provided help from a Pakistani "Samaritan," and brought him safely home.

Mystery Prayer

Almighty Father, your son, Jesus, was already growing "in wisdom and age and favor" when Mary and Joseph finally found him in the Temple. They had been searching for him, and their hearts were full of fear. Jesus said that he needed to be in his "Father's house." Mary, you knew that your son was growing up and that he was beginning to accept his mission. Help me to "let go and let God" work in my life and in those I love. Amen.

Mystery Intentions
- Missing children and young people.
- The grace to "let go and let God. . . ."
- Honor and obedience for parents.
- Your own intention(s).

2. THE LUMINOUS MYSTERIES

——————— *First Luminous Mystery* ———————

THE BAPTISM IN THE JORDAN

Scripture Passage

MATTHEW 3:13-17

Then Jesus came from Galilee to John at the Jordan to be baptized by him. John tried to prevent him, saying, "I need to be baptized by you, and yet you are coming to me?" Jesus said to him in reply, "Allow it now, for thus it is fitting for us to fulfill all righteousness." Then he allowed him. After Jesus was baptized, he came up from the water and behold, the heavens were opened [for him], and he saw the Spirit of God descending like a dove [and] coming upon him. And a voice came from the heavens, saying, "This is my beloved Son, with whom I am well pleased."

Reflection

The Baptism of Jesus seems to be so full of mystery. First of all, there is the mysterious John the Baptist. Scripture reports the amazing promise of his birth and then the holy encounter between his mother, Elizabeth, and Mary, the mother of Jesus. After these passages, however, there is almost no mention of him. He seems to disappear for many years. Some scholars suggest that John may have been a member of the Essenes during these "quiet" years. The Essenes were Jews who lived communally throughout Judea and were dedicated to asceticism, poverty, and abstinence from worldly pleasures, including marriage.

Soon after John came out of the desert, he got everyone's attention. He was probably a startling figure, with shaggy beard and hair. The Gospels report that he was dressed in rough camel-hair clothing and lived on a diet of wild locusts and honey. He was preaching with an intensity that was spellbinding, but frightening as well. Everyone was fascinated with this charismatic but wild holy man. He was calling all Jews to "Repent, for the kingdom of heaven is at hand!" (Matthew 3:2).

All over the country, Israelites were hearing about this fascinating prophet who urged them to confess their sins as they were baptized in the River Jordan. It was a fascinating request. In the practice of Judaism, only newcomers to the faith of the Chosen People were baptized. Nonetheless, from all over Israel, Jews traveled on foot for days to the Jordan. They wanted to hear and consider John's message. Then they plunged into the water to be baptized and to confess their sins. Day after day, week after week, the "revival" continued.

One day, however, Jesus, too, arrived at the banks of the Jordan. Through the Holy Spirit, John the Baptist knew who Jesus was, though they probably hadn't seen each other for many years. John also knew that Jesus was not guilty of any sins. Jesus did not need to repent, and he had no need of baptism.

Jesus saw that John's preaching and baptizing was indeed preparing people for his own ministry. Israel was watching, waiting, and listening. Jesus, the sinless Son of God, wanted to identify himself with the people he had come to redeem. The people were turning to God. Jesus wanted to support this *metanoia* (conversion) among the masses in a very personal way.

This was a defining moment for Jesus of Nazareth.

Although John protested, Jesus insisted on baptism. He went down under the waters of the Jordan River, guided by John's hand upon his head and shoulder. He stood up again a few seconds later, dripping, standing in the bright light of the Judean sun. At that moment, Jesus saw the Spirit of God in the form of a dove coming down toward him. He heard a voice saying, "This is my beloved Son, with whom I am well pleased." John must have seen the Holy Spirit, as well.

The Holy Spirit, Matthew's Gospel suggests, then filled Jesus in a new way. The waters of baptism quickly evaporated from his arms, face, chest, and back. He climbed up the riverbank and back onto the hot, dry road. Jesus knew that his life was changing profoundly. He was led by the Spirit into the desert, where he stayed, prayed, and fasted for forty days. Jesus was preparing for his public life, for the teaching, preaching, healing, and wonder-working that would preoccupy him until the end of his days on earth.

Jesus wanted to identify with those he came to redeem. He wanted to be part of us. Like the hundreds — maybe thousands — of people John had already baptized, Jesus wanted to be washed in the Father's love and in the Spirit's light.

The Rosary in Our Lives

Cleansed and Empowered

Like most Catholics, Bill Kneemiller was baptized in the Catholic community as a baby. He appreciated his solid Catholic upbringing and education in St. Charles, Missouri. But by the time he went to college at the University of Missouri in the early 1970s, he was ready for something new.

"I was intrigued by the philosophy of yoga," he wrote many years later in an article for *The Catholic Messenger*, the diocesan paper of Davenport, Iowa. At the university, he read his first yoga book, *Heaven Lies Within*, and was impressed. He was convinced that he had found a spirituality that fit him perfectly. "After about a year of stumbling around with self-help yoga books, I started practicing the Eastern meditation technique, transcendental meditation."

In fact, Bill's involvement with non-Christian meditation and study continued through his college years. He proudly called himself "a seeker" and occasionally reminded himself that Jesus encouraged disciples to seek spiritual treasures and truth. Bill didn't really want to separate himself from his Christian background. After graduation, however, he traveled to half a dozen countries, studying different meditation techniques. He became a meditation teacher and totally immersed himself in Eastern philosophy and prayer.

Along the way, he met self-help guru Deepak Chopra and heard that even some Trappist monks used Eastern meditation techniques to enrich their own religious expression. It was Bill's understanding that mantras used to chant during meditation were words without specific meanings. "It would be decades," he later admitted, "before I learned that mantras are names of Hindu gods."

By his mid-thirties, Bill Kneemiller realized that something was missing in his life. After eighteen years of involvement with Eastern meditation, he surprised himself. He began attending a family Rosary service. At first, he went out of curiosity — spiritual curiosity, which he always had plenty of. He learned how to meditate on the Rosary prayers and mysteries using the "prayer with the heart" method. "It completely changed my concept that this was just a rote practice." He could see now that the prayer could really be "a conversation and relationship with Christ."

The self-proclaimed seeker made new "Rosary friends" and began going to Catholic conferences and events. He felt a new kinship with Catholics and discovered that the New Age culture and Eastern meditation language began to sound "unusual, even strange." He soon stopped all involvement with it. Privately, however, he wondered if walking away would really be that easy.

His journey back into the heart of Catholicism continued. Deeper "prayer of the heart" through the Rosary also clarified the yearnings of his own heart. Bill soon felt that he had a vocation to the priesthood, and he entered a seminary in Iowa. He was ordained in 1999 and was the only Catholic priest ordained in the entire state of Iowa that year. He took no personal pride in that distinction. He recognized how patiently and lovingly the Mother of God had led him to his calling.

Father Bill Kneemiller, ever the seeker, now directs his curiosity into many areas of Catholic spirituality. In 2010, he attended a conference in Chicago for priests interested in healing. By chance, he met Father Bob Thorn, a diocesan priest from Wisconsin, whose background was surprisingly similar — a former Eastern meditation teacher who had become a priest!

As the two priests traded laughs and stories, Bob Thorn queried his new friend from Iowa. He sensed that Bill still needed to be cleansed and freed from the non-Christian spiritual practices he had once been heavily involved with. Only recently had Bill realized that Eastern mantras were actually chants to Hindu gods. The two priests enlisted the help of several other priests, and Father Bill methodically denounced every Hindu god that is invoked in the meditation ceremony. He proclaimed Jesus Christ as his Savior. "That night," Father Bill wrote, "I slept like a baby." Back in Iowa, he continued to feel lighter, cleansed from New Age practices that had quietly continued to touch his spirit.

Father Bill Kneemiller believes that his discovery of the Rosary and his return to Catholicism were a new beginning for his life. He's immensely grateful that he was washed and renewed. He felt a fresh vitality in his Catholic faith, a new baptism for his priesthood, and a powerful new ministry to the People of God.

Mystery Prayer

Almighty God, Jesus, your "beloved Son," was baptized in the Jordan, just like the thousands of others coming from all over Israel and Judea. Your Holy Spirit filled Jesus in a new way, equipping him for the public life that was beginning. Mary, you knew that Jesus was following his call and beginning the work for which he had been born. Help me to see and embrace my own vocation, and to welcome the special work God gives to me. Amen.

Mystery Intentions

- The baptized and those seeking new life through Baptism.
- Renewal through the Holy Spirit.
- Those seeking a vocation.
- Your own intention(s).

——————— *Second Luminous Mystery* ———————

THE WEDDING FEAST OF CANA

Scripture Passage

JOHN 2:1-11

On the third day there was a wedding in Cana in Galilee, and the mother of Jesus was there. Jesus and his disciples were also invited to the wedding. When the wine ran short, the mother of Jesus said to him, "They have no wine." [And] Jesus said to her, "Woman, how does your concern affect me? My hour has not yet come." His mother said to the servers, "Do whatever he tells you." Now there were six stone water jars there for Jewish ceremonial washings, each holding twenty to thirty gallons. Jesus told them, "Fill the jars with water." So they filled them to the brim. Then he told them, "Draw some out now and take it to the headwaiter." So they took it. And when the headwaiter tasted the water that had become wine, without knowing where it came from (although the servers who had drawn the water knew), the headwaiter called the bridegroom and said to him, "Everyone serves good wine first, and then when people have drunk freely, an inferior one; but you have kept the good wine until now." Jesus did this as the beginning of his signs in Cana in Galilee and so revealed his glory, and his disciples began to believe in him.

Reflection

People who are happily married, or have been, find great joy in the Second Luminous Mystery, the Wedding Feast at Cana. It shows Jesus taking action and working the first miracle of his public life — at a wedding! We see the mother of Jesus intervening to make sure that the joyful celebration of a newly married couple isn't ruined.

The beautiful Gospel story from which this Rosary mystery is drawn appears only in the Gospel of John. John was there at that Cana wedding celebration. He was one of the first apostles called by the Lord. Probably, John, an ex-fisherman, had accompanied several other Galileans who were just beginning to follow Jesus. So, John reported the event just as he saw it unfold — as an eyewitness!

In the midst of a joyous, weeklong wedding celebration, a social calamity began to unfold. To the bride and groom and their families who were hosting this feast, disastrous embarrassment seemed unavoidable. Suddenly, the wine barrels were empty; the wine was gone! In this ancient Middle Eastern culture, showing hospitality to guests was faithfully observed. Failing to feed, entertain, or offer shelter to guests could bring deep and lasting shame on any family.

Some Scripture commentators speculate that either the bride or the groom was closely related to Mary and Jesus. Mary seemed to be more concerned about the looming social catastrophe than would be expected. And so, as John's story tells us, she intervened through Jesus.

Quickly read, the response Jesus made to his mother seems detached, self-centered, and just a bit arrogant. "Woman, how does your concern affect me? My hour has not yet come," Jesus answered. That seems to translate to, "It's not my problem." Instead, scholars of John's Gospel tell us that Christ's words are rich with symbolism, weighted with prophetic allusions to his full mission on earth. Jesus was about to perform a sign, a miracle, but the hour for the ultimate sign — his death and resurrection — had not yet come.

Though she, too, may not have understood the deeper meaning of her son's words, Mary trusted in his goodness. She knew that he would act out of compassion. "Do whatever he tells you," she confidently but discreetly whispered to the servers who were standing nearby. Those words were the last words spoken by Mary in the Gospels.

Jesus, as the Cana story tells us, changed water into wine. Six large stone water jars were soon full of "premium" wine, wine of the very best quality. That meant, some calculate, between 120 and 150 gallons of wine, or the equivalent of about 800 modern bottles! Surely it was much more than the panicked newlyweds could have hoped for — or even needed.

This lavish miracle, worked at a wedding, reminds us of God's overflowing love. In the context of the Luminous Mysteries, we also find a message about marriage. God is ready and willing to do much more than answer the basic needs of married couples and their families. Their unity and joy is precious to him. Our Creator wants to turn water into wine for all of us, but perhaps in a special way for husbands and wives. *He wants to fill them lavishly with transforming love.*

The Rosary in Our Lives

SAVING THE GOOD WINE

In the summer of 1986, Scott Hahn developed the habit of taking solitary walks in his Milwaukee neighborhood just to say his Rosary. Scott knew that it was deeply painful for his wife, Kimberly, to see him holding a Rosary. She had been wounded — in fact, shattered — by his recent conversion to Catholicism.

Scott and Kimberly Hahn had been deeply in love when they married in August 1979. They had also shared a common dream for their married life. They looked forward to serving the Church together — Scott as a Presbyterian minister, and Kimberly directing ministries in whatever congregation they were called to.

Just two weeks after their wedding, Scott began studies at the Gordon Conwell Theological Seminary in Charlotte, North Carolina. Because Scott and Kimberly wanted to study theology "side by side," Kimberly also began taking courses for a master's degree in theology.

Kimberly always knew that Scott had an insatiable interest in theological study. Scott soon came to the conclusion that some fundamental Protestant teachings were false. At the same time, he was buying books about the Catholic Fathers of the Church and still more by Catholic Scripture scholars. There had been a time when Scott believed that "if something is Roman (meaning Roman Catholic), it must be wrong." By 1983 and 1984, that time was over for Scott.

Over the years, Scott had been very honest with his wife about being drawn more and more to Catholicism. In fact, he didn't need to tell her. One evening, Scott admitted that he didn't think he could remain a Presbyterian. Kimberly began to cry. She and Scott now had two little boys to raise — Michael and Gabriel. She didn't want to raise their sons in a family where religious differences would cause confusion and pain. Her father and uncle were Presbyterian ministers. Her brother was studying to become a Presbyterian minister. Scott himself was now a Presbyterian minister and high school teacher in their new home in Fairfax, Virginia. "I don't want to stop being a Presbyterian," Kimberly sobbed.

Just like Kimberly, many of Scott's college and seminary friends were distressed when they heard about his new beliefs. "Are you worshiping Mary yet?" a college friend asked him over the phone. Scott was very aware that Marian doctrines and devotions were among the toughest hurdles for Protestants. However, Scott found that honoring Mary — which was not worshiping her — had solid scriptural roots. He found great peace in praying the Rosary, which honored her.

By 1989, Kimberly was moving down her own bumpy road to Catholicism. During that year, she suffered two miscarriages, one in January and one near the end of the year, shortly before they traveled to the University of Steubenville in Ohio. Scott had a job interview to teach theology at Steubenville. In her grief and pain, she sensed that God was calling her. It was a gentle summons, but it was clear. God wanted her to stop resisting and join Scott.

Kimberly began to find great joy in the Mass with Scott and their children. She became part of an RCIA group and further explored "hurdles" to becoming a Catholic. One by one, the hurdles fell over. On her own, she, too, began to pray and love the Rosary. She saw that Mary, like her own mother, Patricia, could intercede with God for her, because Mary was a loving mother. At the 1990 Easter Vigil, Kimberly became a Catholic.

Scott and Kimberly Hahn realized that God had plans for their ministry together that matched and exceeded the dreams they had had since college. Like the stone jars filled with ordinary water at the wedding feast in Cana, their lives were miraculously transformed and filled to the top. "Do whatever he tells you," Mary had quietly told the servers. At a word from Jesus, the ordinary water had suddenly become the very best wine. The wonderful transformation was much more than the Cana couple could have hoped for.

Mystery Prayer

Loving Creator, it was you who created man and woman in your own image. You gave them to each other in the garden and saw that it was good. You are the author of marriage and family, and their joys and blessings. Mary, you asked Jesus to work his first miracle for newlyweds in Cana. Jesus graciously complied. Help me to ask God to strengthen and bless all married couples and their families. Amen.

Mystery Intentions

- Married couples and those planning to be married.
- For love and joy in relationships.
- Devotion to Mary as an advocate.
- Your own intention(s).

—————— Third Luminous Mystery ——————

THE PROCLAMATION OF THE KINGDOM OF GOD

Scripture Passage

LUKE 4:14-21

Jesus returned to Galilee in the power of the Spirit, and news of him spread throughout the whole region. He taught in their synagogues and was praised by all.

He came to Nazareth, where he had grown up, and went according to his custom into the synagogue on the sabbath day. He stood up to read and was handed a scroll of the prophet Isaiah. He unrolled the scroll and found the passage where it was written:

"The Spirit of the Lord is upon me,
   because he has anointed me
   to bring glad tidings to the poor.
He has sent me to proclaim liberty to captives
   and recovery of sight to the blind,
   to let the oppressed go free,
and to proclaim a year acceptable to the Lord."

Rolling up the scroll, he handed it back to the attendant and sat down, and the eyes of all in the synagogue looked intently at him. He said to them, "Today this scripture passage is fulfilled in your hearing."

Reflection

In writing about the Kingdom of God in his book, *Jesus of Nazareth*, Pope Benedict XVI noted, "The phrase 'Kingdom of God' occurs 122 times in the New Testament as a whole; ninety-nine of these passages are found in the three Synoptic Gospels, and ninety of these ninety-nine texts report words of Jesus."

The pope introduced this stunning statistic by stating that as Jesus announced this new Kingdom of God — his core message — "a milestone is set up in the flow of time; something new takes place. And an answer to this gift is demanded of man; conversion and faith."

In Luke's account of Christ announcing that the Kingdom of God has come to earth, Jesus reads the passage from Isaiah. Everyone in the synagogue listening to him knew that the passage was a prophecy about the coming of the Messiah. When the Messiah came, everything would be different. All of the hurts and miseries of humanity would be healed. Those in prison would be freed, and the poor of the world would hear good and happy news.

Despite the bold proclamation made by Jesus that he was the Messiah and that the Kingdom of God was beginning, few in his own generation could see the truth of it. He did heal many of blindness, paralysis, and deafness. He cast out demons, liberating many from years of torment. He cured lepers — even those who were not Jews — allowing them to return to their families and to life.

But even the followers of Jesus — his disciples — did not really understand that a re-creation of the human condition had begun when he came into the world. Jesus knew that the idea of the Kingdom of God was a mysterious teaching. He talked about it over and over again. It was, and is, a difficult concept.

He constantly chose new images and new stories to teach this large, cosmic truth. The Kingdom is a tiny mustard seed that grows into one of the largest plants. It is so large that even the birds choose to perch in its ample branches. Then again, the Kingdom of God is like yeast that a woman kneads into wheat flour to create dough. Eventually, the dough rises and can be baked to nourish many people. Jesus was trying to tell fishermen, children, and simple village people that God planned a whole new life for them.

Significantly, this Kingdom of God that Jesus spoke about so often is not yet fully established. Scripture scholars say that the term Jesus used about the Kingdom coming is best translated by the words "coming near." The Kingdom of God is coming near or is on the way. It's like the tiny mustard seed and the yeast mixed into the flour.

The establishment and growth of this Kingdom takes time, and it can't be forced or speeded up (almost two thousand years since the life and death of Jesus is not a long period of time in God's eyes). Any kingdom forcefully established or quickly imposed upon us would not be a

Kingdom of God. God's domain offers only love, peace, salvation, forgiveness, and wholeness.

Often, it's very difficult for us to see where the outposts of this Kingdom of God are established today. Our world is still very tortured by the things that Jesus came to heal — poverty, loneliness, sickness, oppression, hatred, selfishness, and on and on. In *Rosarium Virginis Mariae* ("The Rosary of the Virgin Mary"), Pope John Paul II offered a new way of thinking about this Kingdom. He said that the Kingdom really refers to God's saving presence in the world. When Jesus came, God's saving presence was in the world more powerfully than it ever had been before. So, Jesus himself is the most complete sign of the coming Kingdom. As Jesus told Pilate, "My kingdom does not belong to this world" (John 18:36). As Jesus becomes more and more the "King" of our hearts, and the "Lord" of our lives, the Kingdom of God spreads and grows — within us.

The Rosary in Our Lives

SHARING THE GOSPEL ALL OVER THE EARTH

All through the hot, sticky summer months of 1939 and into the autumn, seminarian Patrick Peyton (1909-1992) could hardly get out of his infirmary bed at the University of Notre Dame. He was desperately ill. After so many years of longing to become a priest, the 30-year-old had been just a year away from completing seminary studies and ordination.

The year before, Peyton had been studying theology in Washington, DC, as he prepared to serve as a Holy Cross priest in the foreign missions. He began coughing up enough blood to soak handkerchiefs but denied his illness to himself, and he hid it from everyone else. One night, he hemorrhaged badly and almost died. Doctors in Washington confirmed his worst fears. He had tuberculosis — advanced tuberculosis of the right upper lobe.

Months of treatment back in South Bend, Indiana, near Notre Dame, had not gone well. The wonder drugs that would one day nearly eliminate tuberculosis hadn't been discovered yet. Standard treatment of the disease involved complete rest, a wholesome diet, fresh air, and a lung treatment called pneumothorax. Pneumothorax was the injection of air into the chest cavity, between the lung and chest wall, which forced the collapse of the affected lung. Doctors felt an inactive, "resting" lung was more likely to heal. In young Peyton's case, adhesions to the chest wall prevented the therapeutic lung collapse.

In October, Peyton's doctors suggested a desperate solution to save his life. They would perform three separate surgeries to remove enough ribs in his chest to force his shoulder blade to fall in, collapsing the lung. Tragically, the surgery would also leave him physically disabled. His plans to serve God as a priest, carrying the Gospel to the foreign missions, would be impossible.

Pat Peyton never forgot that night of grief and tears in his Notre Dame dorm room. After a while, he said, he began to think of Jesus on his way to Calvary. He told God that he was willing to share the sufferings of Jesus. He was also willing to accept God's will — whatever it was. The following day, he told his superior about his condition and the awful choice he had to make.

By October 25, news about the Irish seminarian's desperate straits had spread across the campus, reaching Father Cornelius Hagerty. Like Patrick, Father Hagerty had come from Ireland, and he had been Pat's ethics professor. The priest had been impressed with Peyton's keen mind and work ethic. Even more remarkable, however, was the faith and love of God he had seen in Peyton.

"You have the faith, Pat, but you're not using it," Father Hagerty challenged the sad young man stretched out on the dormitory bed. The priest promised to offer a novena of Masses for Patrick. He also told him that he would have to ask Mary to intercede for his own healing. "Our Lady will be as good as you think she is," added Father Hagerty.

The priest's counsel filled Patrick Peyton with new hope and purpose. With the Rosary and other prayers, he began to pray constantly, begging the Mother of God to heal him.

On Halloween, the eve of All Saints' Day, he suddenly felt that she was answering his prayer. "I was eating my supper in bed, and the radio was playing some Irish tunes, transmitted from London," Patrick Peyton later recalled in his autobiography, *All for Her*. "Just then the oppression and the depression and the darkness were swept from my soul, to be replaced by a lightness, a freedom, and a hope."

A week later, the seminarian reported for his medical appointment, although he knew that doctors would find his condition drastically improved. The fluid in his lungs was greatly reduced; clinic personnel were baffled. All through November, the weekly checkups made the good news undeniable. By December 8, the feast of the Immaculate Conception, x-rays and medical tests confirmed the new diagnosis. No sign of tuberculosis!

Within months, Patrick was back in Washington, DC, and back at his theology studies. Because of his medical history, working in the foreign missions was ruled out. Instead, shortly after his ordination on June 15, 1940, he realized in prayer that Mary wanted him to be a different sort of missionary. In 1942, he founded Family Rosary in Albany, New York, and Family Theater Productions in 1947. Father Patrick Peyton, C.S.C., wanted to promote the Rosary and the Gospel through radio and later through television.

During his life, Father Peyton personally proclaimed the Good News and the Kingdom of God around the world.

He addressed twenty-eight million people in Rosary Crusades and many millions more through radio and television. Worldwide, he became known as "the Rosary Priest."

Mystery Prayer

Heavenly Father, you sent Jesus into the world with such Good News! He announced that your Kingdom was being established among us. It meant glad tidings to the poor, liberty to captives, and recovery of sight to the blind. Mary, you must have been so happy that your son's Kingdom work was beginning. Show me where I can help in this Kingdom work — sharing glad tidings and bringing liberty to captives. Amen.

Mystery Intentions

- Acceptance of the Good News of Jesus Christ.
- New evangelization for the world.
- All clergy and ministers of the Word.
- Your own intention(s).

Fourth Luminous Mystery

THE TRANSFIGURATION

Scripture Passage

MARK 9:2-8

After six days Jesus took Peter, James, and John and led them up a high mountain apart by themselves. And he was transfigured before them, and his clothes became dazzling white, such as no fuller on earth could bleach them. Then Elijah appeared to them along with Moses, and they were conversing with Jesus. Then Peter said to Jesus in reply, "Rabbi, it is good that we are here! Let us make three tents: one for you, one for Moses, and one for Elijah." He hardly knew what to say, they were so terrified. Then a cloud came, casting a shadow over them; then from the cloud came a voice, "This is my beloved Son. Listen to him." Suddenly, looking around, they no longer saw anyone but Jesus alone with them.

Reflection

Only the Synoptic Gospels — Matthew, Mark, and Luke — present the brief but beautiful story of the mountaintop transfiguration of Jesus. Some Scripture scholars suggest that John's Gospel did not need to include this story. The fourth Gospel was already full of references to the glory of God in Christ. John, after all, was an eyewitness to the Transfiguration — the only one among the evangelists. John saw Jesus in his shining glory, and the memory of it probably never faded from his mind and heart.

In some ways, this Fourth Luminous Mystery is unique among the mysteries of the Rosary. In it, we do not see what Jesus *does* but who he *is*! All in all, the other mysteries recall events in the life of Jesus or his Blessed Mother, Mary. The Transfiguration of Jesus is a particularly mysterious mystery.

What is a transfigured person? What was it like for Peter, James, and John? They knew Jesus well. They walked the dusty roads of Galilee with him, ate with him, joked with him. But suddenly they saw this same man absolutely glowing with brilliant and beautiful light! It must have been frightening but also thrilling, confusing but also reassuring, inspiring but also humbling.

Did these three men ever talk about this event among themselves or with the other apostles? They must have. How else could anyone begin to process such a breathtaking encounter with God? How else would the Synoptic evangelists have known about it?

We know that the word "transfiguration" has Greek roots and means "metamorphosis" or the transformation into something that's quite different. A monarch butterfly's four-stage development is often used as an example of dramatic metamorphosis in nature. Over a thirty- to forty-day period, the butterfly's fertilized egg develops into a larva (or caterpillar), and then forms a chrysalis (or cocoon). Then, after silent, hidden development in the chrysalis, the beautiful butterfly emerges — ready to take flight, and delighted, somehow, that its sluggish days on the ground are over.

But that's not the way to see the Transfiguration of Jesus. The Lord was transfigured but not transformed. Jesus did not evolve through developmental stages to become something different. During the Transfiguration, Jesus was the same as he always was — the son of Mary *and* the only Son of God. Suddenly his divine and radiant identity was visible and gloriously manifested for his three closest friends.

In our own lives, there are times when we catch a little glimmer of what the Transfiguration must have meant for Peter, James, and John. We get a quick peek at God's glory, his shining truth, and his overwhelming love. Such moments are so clear, so bright, and so endearing. We often remember these moments for a lifetime; they can easily bring us to tears. Reflections of God's glory could come as you watch a perfect sunset, witness the birth of a child, or see the wind gently rippling golden wheat beneath a cloudless blue sky.

The wonderful lesson in the Transfiguration of Jesus is that God the Father wanted to do more than simply tell us about Jesus. God wanted to show us the glorious and shining truth about his Son. As Peter said in his second epistle, he personally witnessed the Transfiguration of Jesus, which St. Thomas Aquinas later called "the greatest miracle."

Peter suggests that we keep our eyes trained on that glorious light, Jesus, the Light of the World.

"You will do well," he said, "to be attentive to it, as to a lamp shining in a dark place, until day dawns and the morning star rises in your hearts" (2 Peter 1:19).

The Rosary in Our Lives
TOTALLY TRANSFORMED

When Brian Pessaro of Temple Trace, Florida, finally got around to telling about his own transformation — through the Rosary — he was refreshingly blunt. Pessaro is much too young to have watched Archbishop Fulton Sheen, the iconic Catholic TV evangelist who was immensely popular during the 1950s and 1960s. But Pessaro had read a few things about Fulton Sheen. The archbishop once described the Rosary as the "perfect prayer" because it took nineteen minutes to pray. Reportedly, nineteen minutes was the maximum amount of time that the average person could remain attentive.

"The Rosary is excruciating," Pessaro argues, contradicting the great archbishop. By that, he means "excruciatingly difficult" and "a real chore" to pray well. Nonetheless, Brian has learned to love and pray the Rosary on a daily basis.

"I've often flopped into bed late at night, only to realize I hadn't done it yet," Brian writes. "I groan as I slide out from the sheets and reach for my beads on the nightstand. Those next nineteen minutes are a far cry from the 'perfect prayer' Archbishop Sheen described. I can barely keep my eyes opened, much less my mind focused. To be honest, it's not much easier when I'm wide awake. I stink at contemplating the mysteries."

Despite the hurdles, Brian persists and stays the course with the Rosary because "I wouldn't be where I am today had it not been for Mary's intercession." It was the Rosary, he says, that helped free him from a nineteen-year addiction to pornography.

Brian knows how it all began. When he was eleven, his best friend's father had a stack of *Playboy* magazines in the basement. The boys found plenty of reason to spend time in the basement, and soon Brian was "hooked." All through his teenage years, into young adulthood, and even as a married man, Brian found that he couldn't resist pornography. By the age of twenty-five, he was satisfying his craving with Internet porn.

"I was so hooked on Internet porn," he says, "that I would itch for my wife to leave the apartment so I could secretly jump online." It wasn't that Brian didn't feel any guilt or shame about his problem. He tried several times to stop, but his fixation got even worse.

Then, a friend of Brian's who knew nothing about his addiction gave him a book about the alleged apparitions of Mary at Medjugorje. Brian read the book and found himself deeply touched. He felt as if Mary reached up from the pages and grabbed him by the collar. "I felt her say to me sternly, 'Brian you've got to stop looking at that garbage. Starting now!' "

Brian wondered how he was to stop. He turned the page of the book and saw that, at Medjugorje, Mary was urging pilgrims to pray the Rosary and wear a scapular. He wasn't too sure what a scapular was but groaned at the thought of praying the Rosary. Every time he had tried to pray it in the past, he had given it up — "so boring!"

Brian distinctly felt that Mary wasn't taking no for an answer. He went to his computer and ordered a scapular. Then he remembered that his grandmother's rosary had been in his dresser for years. He went and got the rosary. That night and the next night and the night after that, Brian Pessaro dropped to his knees on the bedroom floor and prayed the Rosary. Weeks, then months, and then years passed. Brian stayed with the Rosary, but his addiction left.

A total transformation! Brian says that praying the Rosary each day has transformed his life. He can now see things as he never saw them before. There's plenty of joy and light in his spirit that wasn't there before. It wasn't just that he "kicked a nasty porn habit." The compulsion to view pornography completely vanished from his life that first night! Brian has read about what pornography does to the brain. The instantaneous disappearance of a nineteen-year pornography addiction is nothing short of a miracle. It is Mary's gift to him.

Mystery Prayer

Almighty God, you showed the magnificent and shining glory of your divine Son, Jesus, to Peter, James, and John. Jesus was transfigured before their eyes. Those three apostles saw him, as he truly is — the Son of God. Their faith was strengthened, and their hearts were moved. Mary, you didn't need to see your son shining with light to know who he was. On the days when my faith needs support, help me remember that he is my God. He shines with a blinding and unforgettable light. Amen.

Mystery Intentions

- Recognition that Jesus is God.
- Seeing God's hidden glory in creation.
- Those in need of personal transformation.
- Your own intention(s).

——— Fifth Luminous Mystery ———

THE INSTITUTION OF THE EUCHARIST

Scripture Passage

Luke 22:14-20

When the hour came, he took his place at table with the apostles. He said to them, "I have eagerly desired to eat this Passover with you before I suffer, for, I tell you, I shall not eat it [again] until there is fulfillment in the kingdom of God." Then he took a cup, gave thanks, and said, "Take this and share it among yourselves; for I tell you [that] from this time on I shall not drink of the fruit of the vine until the kingdom of God comes." Then he took the bread, said the blessing, broke it, and gave it to them, saying, "This is my body, which will be given for you; do this in memory of me." And likewise the cup after they had eaten, saying, "This cup is the new covenant in my blood, which will be shed for you."

Reflection

Down through the centuries of the Church, many saints wrote about the Eucharist as their source of both spiritual food and spiritual light. Undoubtedly, they often read this passage from Luke about the institution of the Eucharist. Perhaps, however, they sometimes wondered what Jesus could have meant when he held up the flat Passover bread, blessed it, tore it, and began handing pieces of it to the apostles gathered around him.

"This is my body, which will be given for you," he said slowly and deliberately, even as he watched the eyes of his apostles filling with surprise and then confusion.

In the Catholic celebration of the Eucharist, we believe that the bread and wine is truly the Body and Blood of Jesus. We believe it because Jesus promised it would be so. We call this core teaching about the Eucharist "the real presence." Because Jesus is God, his will and words must be rooted in truth. Jesus wouldn't and couldn't make a promise that wouldn't be true.

So, Jesus gave himself as "the bread of life" to his friends at the Last Supper. He also gave himself as "the bread of life" to everyone who would later be his followers. St. Faustina Kowalska (1905-1938), the Polish mystic and "apostle of Divine Mercy," called the Eucharist "the Bread of the Strong." Century after century, Jesus has stayed with us, giving us the best food of all for the journey of life. What an amazing journey of light it has been for the followers of Jesus.

Writing early in the fifth century, St. John Chrysostom (c. 347-407), a Father of the Church, explained that the power of the priest presiding at the Eucharistic celebration came from God alone. "The priest standing there in the place of Christ says these words," St. John said, "but their power and grace are from God. 'This is My Body,' he says, and these words transform what lies before him."

St. Francis of Assisi (1181-1226) was deeply devoted to the Eucharist and Eucharistic Adoration. In a prayer written shortly before his death, he pleaded with his Franciscan brothers to draw strength from Jesus in the little white host. "Brothers, look at the humility of God, and pour out your hearts before him!" he wrote. "Humble yourselves that you may be exalted by Him! Hold back nothing of yourselves for yourselves, that He who gives Himself totally to you may receive you totally!"

Many centuries later, on an island in the South Pacific in the Kingdom of Hawaii, a Belgian priest relied on the Body and Blood of Jesus to help sustain him. St. Damien de Veuster ministered alone to lepers isolated on Molokai, where they had been sent to die. In addition to serving as their pastor, Father Damien was also their doctor, counselor, handyman, and friend.

"Without the constant presence of our Divine Master upon the altar in my poor chapels, I never could have persevered casting my lot with the afflicted of Molokai; the foreseen consequence of which begins now to appear on my skin and is felt throughout the body," he wrote to his superiors back in Belgium. In 1885, he announced to his congregation of lepers, "I am one of you." Even as his illness progressed, he continued to build hospitals, clinics, and churches, and some six hundred coffins.

Many Christians have come to understand what Jesus meant when he shared wine and bread and gave these common elements a whole new meaning. The first followers of

Jesus found — as have many others throughout Christian history — that their hearts "understood" the Eucharist before their minds did. Our hearts are won over by a God who loves us so much that he feeds us forever, and simply refuses to be separated from us.

The Rosary in Our Lives

OUR DAILY BREAD

Only three days after the stock market crash in October 1929, the Capuchins opened a soup kitchen at St. Bonaventure Monastery on Mt. Elliott Avenue in Detroit. It was a providential initiative. As the months moved along, the Great Depression hit Detroit harder than any other large industrial American city.

None of the Capuchin priests and brothers at St. Bonaventure knew more about the city's agony than Father Solanus Casey, O.F.M. Cap. (1870-1957). The sixty-year-old Father Solanus was the monastery's porter. For years, however, the priest's ministry had gone way beyond his assignment — meeting and greeting visitors at the monastery door. Many years before, people discovered that this Irish priest from Wisconsin was always willing to listen to their troubles. He also had extraordinary spiritual gifts of discernment, prophecy, and healing. When people asked Father Solanus to pray for healings, they were often healed!

Father Solanus never took credit for any healing or "miraculous" events reported by monastery visitors. Solanus explained that God loves us like a doting father. He told people that God really wants to answer all of our needs. It was obvious to those who came to visit him that Father Solanus was a man of prayer. Once the last visitors left at 10:30 or 11 p.m., the doorkeeper would head for the chapel to spend hours in prayer. Solanus was also deeply devoted to the Rosary and said he owed his vocation to the Blessed Virgin.

As the Great Depression deepened, the monastery soup kitchen was feeding as many as three thousand people a day. They were mostly men who had lost jobs, homes, and often hope as well. The Capuchins were worried. Providing enough food was difficult — especially since it was impossible to predict how many people would be lining up on the street for the bread, soup, and coffee the kitchen offered. Everyone was afraid that a day might come when the monastery would have to turn away hungry people.

Father Solanus was constantly phoning the wealthy and influential people he knew in Detroit to ask for help with food. He arranged for volunteers to take a pickup truck and go out on "begging trips" to area farms. Every donated bushel of potatoes or onions helped. Father Solanus also urged everyone to "trust in the good God" and in the Blessed Virgin Mary.

One day, however, Father Herman Buss ran back to the monastery from the kitchen. He had completely run out of bread. Father Herman thought that perhaps Father Solanus could quickly call one of his well-to-do "connections" for immediate help. Two hundred or three hundred men were waiting in the dining area for a meal.

Fingering his rosary, the doorkeeper hurried back to the dining room with Father Herman to reassure the worried men.

"Just wait and God will provide," Father Solanus told them. "Now, let's say the Our Father. . . ."

Fathers Solanus and Herman had just turned around after the Our Father when a bakery truck pulled up near the soup kitchen's front door. A deliveryman hauled in a heavy basket full of bread. He had a truckload of food for the kitchen, he told the priests. As the deliveryman carted in basket after basket of food, tears rolled down the faces of many of the hungry men. The room was quiet as the platters of bread and bowls of soup began to circulate. Right before their eyes, God was giving them their "daily bread."

"See, God provides," smiled Father Solanus Casey, as he moved around the room, patting men on the back and asking if they wanted coffee or water. "Nobody will starve as long as you put your confidence in God, in Divine Providence."

His face said it all. He hadn't seemed surprised at all by the sudden appearance of a truckload of food.

Mystery Prayer

God, your son, Jesus, deeply loved his brothers and sisters and wanted to remain with them until the end of time. So, he gave them his Body and Blood under the appearance of bread and wine. He remained with his first disciples, and he remains with us in the Eucharist. Mary, you understood the boundless love of your son. Remind me to cherish the Eucharist. Don't let me take this "bread of life" for granted. Amen.

Mystery Intentions

- Love of Jesus in the Eucharist.
- A growing commitment to feed the hungry.
- "Food" for those with spiritual hungers.
- Your own intention(s).

3. THE SORROWFUL MYSTERIES

--------- *First Sorrowful Mystery* ---------

THE AGONY IN THE GARDEN

Scripture Passage

MARK 14:32-42

Then they came to a place named Gethsemane, and he said to his disciples, "Sit here while I pray." He took with him Peter, James, and John, and began to be troubled and distressed. Then he said to them, "My soul is sorrowful even to death. Remain here and keep watch." He advanced a little and fell to the ground and prayed that if it were possible the hour might pass by him; he said, "Abba, Father, all things are possible to you. Take this cup away from me, but not what I will but what you will." When he returned he found them asleep. He said to Peter, "Simon, are you asleep? Could you not keep watch for one hour? Watch and pray that you may not undergo the test. The spirit is willing but the flesh is weak." Withdrawing again, he prayed, saying the same thing. Then he returned once more and found them asleep, for they could not keep their eyes open and did not know what to answer him. He returned a third time and said to them, "Are you still sleeping and taking your rest? It is enough. The hour has come. Behold, the Son of Man is to be handed over to sinners. Get up, let us go. See, my betrayer is at hand."

Reflection

In Luke's account of the agony of Jesus, the evangelist says, "When he rose from prayer and returned to his disciples, he found them sleeping from grief" (Luke 22:45).

Most of us pause a bit at that implicit criticism of Peter, James, and John. We know that Jesus was suffering the deepest agony and spending his last night on earth. So how could his closest friends fall asleep? In some ways, we are terribly shocked. How could three grown men fail Jesus in his hour of greatest need? And yet, we are sympathetic too. Peter, James, and John were feeling helpless, despondent, and were overwhelmed with grief and emotional exhaustion. Though they tried hard not to, each one of them surrendered to the merciful and private oblivion that sleep gives us.

Jesus was deeply wounded by the weakness of his best friends. All three of the Synoptic Gospels make that clear. These men were his most trusted disciples. His sense of abandonment must have been almost unbearable. No one on earth offered him the comfort and support he needed.

After more than twenty centuries, it can be difficult to really grasp the pain Jesus endured in Gethsemane. We're tempted to think, "Well, he was God. It was much easier for him to be strong, brave, and loving. And Jesus didn't have to wonder whether he would truly rise again after this terrible trial."

It's true. Jesus was and is God. But being God did not diminish his humanity. He was fully divine *and* fully human. As the author of Hebrews says, Jesus was like us, "tested in every way, yet without sin" (Hebrews 4:15). During his passion, Jesus really was horribly tested in every way — emotionally, psychologically, and physically. And during that long and lonely night beneath the massive olive trees in the Garden of Gethsemane, he sobbed uncontrollably. His body became soaked with nervous sweat; he shook with fear and bewilderment.

Why was his Father asking him to suffer in this way? Every first-century Jew knew about the cruelty of Roman execution on the cross. Not only was crucifixion an agonizing way to die, but it was also designed to humiliate and demean its naked victims. They were left to die in stupefying pain on public crosses. Birds and animals came to feed off the rotting bodies of the crucified.

In his mind's eye, Jesus, the Son of God, foresaw his suffering and death. What a heart-stopping nightmare he envisioned. In his humanity, Jesus wondered why he should endure this kind of suffering and death. "Abba, Father, all things are possible to you. Take this cup away from me," Jesus prayed, adding, "but not what I will but what you will" (Mark 14:26).

Jesus had spent three selfless, homeless years teaching, healing, and casting out demons. He had traveled all over Israel sharing the Good News — the best news ever shared anywhere at any time. Jesus taught about his loving Father to help people understand that God was also their loving Father. Jesus told people that he had come to save them from nothing less than sin and death.

Mel Gibson's film, *The Passion of the Christ*, chronicles, in excruciatingly vivid detail, the punishment endured by Jesus in his last day of life. It is a hard but important film for those who want to really understand what happened to Jesus. But Father Ronald Rolheiser, O.M.I., a theologian and best-selling Catholic author, has said that the physical suffering endured by Jesus is not what the evangelists wanted us to keep in mind.

"They emphasize," wrote Father Rolheiser, "[that] he was alone, betrayed, humiliated, hung out to dry. Nobody stood up for him" (*Catholic Update*, February 2008). The agony of Jesus was so much more terrible because he had no one to console and comfort him.

The worst part of his agony was suffering all alone. The tragic predictions of the prophet Isaiah, written eight hundred years before the birth of the Messiah, came to pass:

> He was spurned and avoided by men,
>   a man of suffering, knowing pain,
> Like one from whom you turn your face,
>   spurned, and we held him in no esteem. (Isaiah 53:3)

The Rosary in Our Lives

A Nation in Agony

Early one March morning in 1980, on a day that was already growing hot and sticky, Archbishop Oscar Arnulfo Romero (1917-1980) of San Salvador walked out of the little three-room hermitage where he lived and locked the door behind him. This very modest "bishop's residence" was on the grounds of Divine Providence Hospital. He was very comfortable in this bungalow.

Romero had just finished early morning prayers. He shoved his hand down inside the side pocket of his white cassock to make sure that his Rosary was there. Devoted to the Rosary ever since boyhood, he found peace and consolation reflecting on the sequence of the Joyful, Sorrowful, and Glorious mysteries. Throughout the day, the sixty-two-year-old bishop would finger the beads down in his pocket, reconnecting with the peace he found with it.

Every day now, the archbishop saw El Salvador living out sorrowful mysteries. His people were being tortured, demeaned, and forced to carry the heavy cross of oppression. And yes, there were also those who were being unjustly condemned and executed. Some reports said that three thousand people were murdered each month. Many tortured bodies were left in the city dumps. The people of El Salvador were suffering one long "agony in the garden." The man who had become their voice sensed that their suffering — and his own — would certainly increase.

By personality, the archbishop of San Salvador had always been high strung and very vulnerable to stress. Oscar Romero recognized that. He also knew that he had plenty of reasons to feel abandoned and anguished. As he tried to speak out each day for the rights of the poor in El Salvador, he had almost no support from those in power.

A majority of the nation's landowners had no intention of supporting workers' rights. Romero started to champion the *campesinos* soon after he became San Salvador's archbishop in 1977. Economic exploitation was widespread on the coffee estates and on the plantations where sugar and cotton were grown. Malnutrition — especially among children — was slowly draining the life out of his people. And to stifle any political reform or change, the military regime in El Salvador kidnapped, tortured, exiled, or murdered those working for social justice.

Most disturbing of all had been the fact that even the papal nuncio and most of his brother bishops also abandoned him. In fact, the bishops wrote to Rome, complaining that he was becoming a celebrity. He was intervening in politics too much. The archbishop understood that the bishops and the political establishment were upset by his newfound commitment to the poor. When he became archbishop in 1977, he was theologically and politically conservative, and totally disconnected from politics.

Three weeks after he became archbishop, however, his Jesuit friend, Father Rutilio Grande, was murdered along with an elderly man and a boy. The man and boy had committed the "crime" of offering the priest a ride. When Romero saw his friend's bloody and lifeless body, he was overwhelmed. There was grief but also a quiet shift in his spirit. He saw instantly that God was calling him now to become a different kind of shepherd. He had to respond to the rampant violence and injustice by preaching the Gospel.

For almost three years, the archbishop arranged to have his Sunday homilies broadcast over the diocesan radio station. Thousands of ordinary people all over the country had grown to love him. He showed them how the Gospel applied to their everyday lives. He assured them of God's love.

As he crossed the hospital courtyard and made his way down the street, he was also soon reminded that some of his countrymen really hated him. On one of the cars conspicuously parked near the archdiocesan office building, he noticed a new bumper sticker: "Be a Patriot; Kill a Priest."

The archbishop stopped for a moment to study the car. He shook his head at the spirit of violence that was infecting the country he loved. Reaching for his rosary again, down inside his pocket, he walked up the steps toward his office to begin another busy day. On March 24, 1980, Archbishop Romero was assassinated while celebrating the evening Mass in the chapel of Divine Providence Hospital.

Mystery Prayer

Merciful God, Jesus, your Son, was beginning the agonizing journey to his cruel and painful death. He knew that all along the way, there would be terrifying pain. Jesus asked to be spared from a horrible death on the cross, but he also promised to do your will. Mary, surely you knew that the suffering of Jesus was beginning. Strengthen me in times of anxiety, stress, fear, and loneliness. Help me to do God's will, even when it hurts to do so. Amen.

Mystery Intentions

- Those suffering mental and emotional stress.
- People who feel abandoned or lonely.
- Courage and faith in the midst of great suffering.
- Your own intention(s).

——— Second Sorrowful Mystery ———

THE SCOURGING AT THE PILLAR

Scripture Passage

MARK 15:13-15

They shouted again, "Crucify him." Pilate said to them, "Why? What evil has he done?" They only shouted the louder, "Crucify him." So Pilate, wishing to satisfy the crowd, released Barabbas to them and, after he had Jesus scourged, handed him over to be crucified.

Reflection

In modern national and international parlance, "cruel and unusual punishment" is a phrase used to describe criminal punishment that's unacceptable because of the suffering endured by the one being punished.

During the writing of the first ten amendments to the U.S. Constitution, the wording about "cruel and unusual" punishment was borrowed almost word for word from the 1689 English Bill of Rights. So, the Eighth Amendment to the Constitution of the United States read, "Excessive bail shall not be required, nor excessive fines imposed, nor cruel and unusual punishments inflicted."

In recent years, this amendment has been legally invoked to challenge or overturn some methods of legal execution in individual states. The legal rationale is that human beings should not be forced to endure cruel procedures, even during an execution that is taking their lives.

No such humanitarian concerns preoccupied the ancient world. In that world, Jesus and many others were killed in a way that was extraordinarily cruel. Roman crucifixion imposed excruciating suffering. But scourging typically preceded crucifixion. It was intended to humiliate the victim and hasten his death through blood loss and shock from the pain.

A flagellum was a short Roman whip with small iron balls and sharpened pieces of sheep bone attached to leather strips. The flagellum was used to whip the naked prisoner. His hands were tied to a ring at the top of a pillar. The Gospels do not report how many separate blows Jesus received at the Praetorium, where he was also condemned to death. Jewish law required that a scourging not exceed thirty-nine blows. Some Scripture scholars believe that the scourging Jesus received was particularly severe. They contend that the Roman soldiers ignored the Jewish limit on blows. Two soldiers took turns whipping. Or, if just one soldier was using the flagellum, he alternated positions so that both sides of the victim's body were equally bruised and viciously lacerated. By the end of the scourging, the victim's shoulders, back, and buttocks were covered with deep, bleeding stripes of ragged flesh.

Jesus was probably unconscious or in a pre-shock state when the brutal scourging finally ended. The punishment Jesus had endured in the previous ten to twelve hours — in addition to the deprivation of food, water, and sleep — also contributed to his vulnerability. From a medical perspective, the physical condition of Jesus was "serious" and possibly "critical." Nonetheless, the soldiers threw water on him to revive him and untied his hands from the scourging pillar.

As soon as Jesus was painfully hauled to his feet, his hands were bound together again. Those who had beaten him began to taunt him. But they also sat him down nearby to wait. Orders had not yet been given to take the condemned to Golgotha, the execution site outside the city walls.

Roman and Jewish authorities might have been worried that the Galilean's supporters would be organizing a rebellion. The Romans had heard that Jesus had a large following and many disciples. The Jews knew that thousands had followed Jesus to hear him preach and teach all over Judea. Everyone had heard testimonies about the way he had multiplied bread and fish to feed thousands of people. Stories about the more recent raising of Lazarus from the dead in nearby Bethany were still circulating. Why wouldn't there be an uprising to save this man?

Over the centuries, Israel had known many prophets who had excited the masses with messages and gifts. But none had been like Jesus of Nazareth.

Jesus waited in the Praetorium, panting and ready to scream with the pain he felt from every inch of his back, legs, arms, and shoulders. Meanwhile, Roman soldiers were out walking through Jerusalem's stone-paved streets, pushing back crowds and shouting warnings as many people wept.

The Rosary in Our Lives

SUFFERING FOR SINS

Ten-year-old Jacinta Marto (1910-1920) was trying to lie very still on her bed in the isolation ward of Estefania Hospital in Lisbon, Portugal. Every time she moved even a little bit, waves of pain from wounds and an abscess on her side made her cry out in pain. Even though there was no one nearby to hear her, the youngest visionary of Fátima wished to suffer this torture in silence. Every moment of suffering and every Rosary bead she prayed were offered now for the reparation of sins.

In the fall and winter months of 1918, Jacinta had developed purulent pleurisy. Later, she also contracted tuberculosis. Two ribs had recently been removed to help the doctors drain her lungs of fluid. When the bandages of all of these wounds were changed, it felt like she was being flayed alive.

Jacinta, her brother Francisco, and their cousin Lucia dos Santos were the three young visionaries of apparitions of Our Lady at Fátima in 1917. Her father, Tito Marto, always called Jacinta "the sweetest" of his children. She loved to dance and talk. Sometimes, her family hoped that the little chatterbox would be more like Francisco. He was reserved, contemplative, loyal, and a steady worker.

Now, the little girl was separated from her family, who lived in the tiny village of Aljustrel, near Fátima. Jacinta missed all of her family, but she missed her brother Francisco most of all. Francisco was almost eleven when he died the previous April of bronchial pneumonia. She, Francisco, and Lucia had all seen the Angel of Peace in 1916, and the Blessed Virgin Mary in 1917. The Virgin had told the children that Jacinta and Francisco would die soon after the apparitions. Lucia was to live a long life in order to share the Fátima messages with the world.

Jacinta was very confident that Francisco was smiling at her from his place in heaven. Nonetheless, she was still very lonely. She also knew that she would be all alone at the moment of her death. Our Lady had told her that.

When the pain was not so bad, Jacinta thought back to the sunny, happy days she once spent with Francisco and Lucia. The three — the youngest children in their large families — were given the job of tending the family flocks. In the morning, they would meet and drive the sheep out to graze on the Cova da Ira property that Lucia's father owned. Once the sheep were settled in the field, there was time to play. The three often fashioned "houses" by piling up dead tree branches and dragging rocks together to form the perimeter of the walls of a "house."

Jacinta also played with the sheep. She named them and especially loved to hold the lambs in her lap. One evening as they drove the flocks back to the village, she tried to carry a lamb over her small shoulder, just like Jesus, the Good Shepherd, in a picture she had seen. Francisco and Lucia laughed and laughed as Jacinta struggled to keep the frisky lamb balanced on her shoulder.

By noon, it was often hot. The young shepherds would then find some shade and eat their lunches. They rested a bit, taking turns checking on the sheep.

Each day after lunch, they prayed a shortcut version of the Rosary. They said just the words "Our Father" and "Hail Mary," without reciting the full prayers. Jacinta smiled when she recalled that after the Angel of Peace appeared to them, they began to pray the full Rosary every day. The angel, a handsome young man shining with light, had taught them how to pray the Rosary properly. He also asked them to make sacrifices, as reparation for the sins of the world, so they often fed their lunches to the sheep.

Jacinta's thin face grimaced as another wave of pain washed over her. She knew, however, that her suffering would soon end. She died — all alone — on February 20, 1920. Earlier in the day, she had asked to receive the Eucharist and to be anointed. Jacinta Marto and her brother Francisco Marto were both beatified in 2000, the Jubilee Year, by Pope John Paul II.

Mystery Prayer

God, Our Father, Jesus was so cruelly beaten and abused. So much pain was inflicted upon him. He struggled bravely to stand and take it. Roman soldiers merely carried out what the people of Jerusalem had asked for — the vicious and cruel scourging of an innocent man headed for the cross. Mary, every blow Jesus received must have wounded your poor heart. Support and fortify me when unavoidable suffering and pain come my way. Show me how to help and pray for others who are suffering. Amen.

Mystery Intentions

- People suffering physical pain.
- An end to physical violence and torture.
- Compassion and justice for prisoners.
- Your own intention(s).

Third Sorrowful Mystery

THE CROWNING WITH THORNS

Scripture Passage

MATTHEW 27:27-31

Then the soldiers of the governor took Jesus inside the praetorium and gathered the whole cohort around him. They stripped off his clothes and threw a scarlet military cloak about him.

Weaving a crown out of thorns, they placed it on his head, and a reed in his right hand. And kneeling before him, they mocked him, saying, "Hail, King of the Jews!" They spat upon him and took the reed and kept striking him on the head. And when they had mocked him, they stripped him of the cloak, dressed him in his own clothes, and led him off to crucify him.

Reflection

Why did Roman soldiers mock and torture Jesus, a bleeding, pitiful figure who was obviously wracked with pain? The brutal scourging that Jesus received was routinely given to prisoners about to be executed. But there was no Roman directive about taunting and humiliating a man whose "worst" crime seemed to be challenging the Jewish establishment. Jesus was already a "dead man walking."

What sort of cheap sport did the Roman soldiers find in wounding Jesus with a painful crown of thorns? Why would they humiliate him with insults and a "king's" cloak thrown over his bleeding back and shoulders? These Romans had no interest in Jewish politics.

The likeliest answer is that these soldiers were simply amusing themselves as some of their comrades finished gathering what was needed for the crucifixion. One commentator suggests that the soldiers were likely part of Pilate's bodyguard. If so, they had accompanied the prefect of the Roman province of Judea from Caesarea on the Mediterranean. They weren't familiar with what was happening in Jerusalem and why some Jews insisted that Pilate execute Jesus.

Once in Jerusalem, however, they may have heard a bit of gossip about the "Kingdom of God" that the Galilean rabbi preached about. But kingdoms have to have kings to rule them. The bruised and bloodied man's situation must have struck them as "funny," in an ironic way. If Jesus was any king at all, he was certainly a pathetic one. He didn't look as though he had ever been a threat to Roman authority and power.

Continuing their fun, the soldiers looked around to find "kingly" garb and a crown for Jesus. It's likely that one of them cut off some branches of a thorny bush now known as Euphorbia milii, or the Crown of Thorns plant. The plant, native to Madagascar, had been brought to the Middle East before the time of Christ.

Cutting and twisting the pliable but thorny branches with care, the soldiers fashioned a sort of cap or helmet. To avoid getting pricked, they certainly used a heavy cloak or cape to pick it up and push it firmly and cruelly down upon the head of Jesus. He must have gasped in pain as this agonizing crown pierced his forehead and head with dozens of painful thorns. Blood from dozens of wounds ran down his face, stinging his eyes and finding its salty way into his mouth.

A soldier's red cloak was then thrown around the shoulders and back of the squirming, moaning man, whose hands were tied. By then, the Roman soldiers had their "king." So, we can envision the openhanded slaps, the beatings, and the taunting words growing more and more vicious: "How do you like your crown, O King? Here's your royal robe, Your Highness. You are so magnificent, O Great King!"

It's not too hard to imagine what these hardened Roman soldiers would have said to the suffering man. They had no personal grudge or hatred for the one they were killing. They simply had no respect for his human dignity, no sympathy for his pain, and no qualms about the job they did with brutality.

And Jesus?

Surely, Jesus teetered on the brink of unconsciousness again. Perhaps he searched for a way to climb out of this pit of pain through the psalms, which he had known since boyhood:

> Even though I walk through the valley of the shadow
>   of death,
>   I will fear no evil, for you are with me;
>   your rod and your staff comfort me.
> You set a table before me
>   in front of my enemies;
> You anoint my head with oil;
>   my cup overflows.
> Indeed, goodness and mercy will pursue me
>   all the days of my life;
> I will dwell in the house of the LORD
>   for endless days. (Psalm 23:4-6)

The Rosary in Our Lives

NOT IN THIS WORLD

On October 30, 1867, twenty-three-year-old Sister Marie-Bernard (Bernadette Soubirous: 1844-1879) was bubbling over with joy. With forty-three other nuns, Bernadette, the only visionary of Lourdes, was making her solemn profession with the Sisters of Charity at Nevers in France.

It had been nine years since the petite, pretty, miller's daughter welcomed the visits of the stunning, beautiful Virgin. The Virgin came to visit Bernadette in a rock grotto at Lourdes. Bernadette had been a teenager, a sickly girl already weighed down with severe asthma and extreme poverty. She was, nonetheless, cheerful, even-tempered and full of fun. Because of illness in her early childhood and poor nutrition, Bernadette's growth had been stunted. She was only four feet eight inches tall.

Since Lourdes, there had been many torturous and humiliating trials. Initially, no one believed her reports about the apparitions of a beautiful woman who smiled and prayed the Rosary with her. However, a miraculous stream bubbled and then gushed up at the base of the grotto. Healings began to be reported.

After that, no one would leave her alone. People flocked to the drab, dank Soubirous house and begged "the saint" to bless their rosaries. "I'm not a priest!" she shouted, frustrated and burdened. As the years went by, it only grew worse. She despised her "celebrity" status because no one treated her as a unique individual, with her own feelings and goals.

A young medical student who had never met Bernadette asked the bishop of Bernadette's diocese for his permission to marry her. He threatened to kill himself if she refused. She could hardly wait to escape and finally decided which religious congregation to join. Dozens of orders from all over France had "recruited" her, hoping to acquire "the visionary of Lourdes."

"Handling" the visionary had proved difficult for Sister Marie-Bernard's superiors. Mother Marie-Therese Vazou, the mistress of novices, had been excited about Bernadette's coming to Nevers. But when she finally met her, this novice mistress from a wealthy and cultured French family was deeply disappointed. In fact, she was disgusted! Even though Bernadette was clearly very pious, Mother Marie-Therese saw that Bernadette came from a poor, working-class family. She was ignorant and stubborn, and she had a worldly sense of humor. How could the Virgin Mother of God choose such a short, crude, unlikable peasant girl?

Mother Marie-Therese believed it was her job to take Bernadette down a peg or two. She was offended that the Lourdes visionary politely refused to share any secrets from the Virgin. She described the girl as a "stiff, very touchy character." Bernadette needed to be humbled, corrected. Mother Marie-Therese convinced the other religious superiors that her approach was best for Bernadette's spiritual welfare. Bernadette should not be allowed to believe that she was closer to God than anyone else.

Little Sister Marie-Bernard knew none of these pastoral policies as she waited with her peers on Profession Day in October 1867. One by one, her fellow nuns rose as their names were called. They went to the bishop, knelt, and received their assignments, or "obediences," from him. Her name was not called. "I would have really liked to do as everyone else," she whispered tearfully to a friend.

Just then, the bishop called her name in a tone that suggested that she had been forgotten and then suddenly remembered.

"Is it true, Sister Marie-Bernard, that you are good for nothing?" he said aloud for all to hear.

"Yes, it is true," she said quietly, thinking that he was referring to her fragile health.

He left her kneeling there, waiting, hands folded in prayer. Her friends could see that she was clearly wounded by her status as "the useless" sister. Even though her assignment had already been carefully discussed and decided upon, the bishop played his role. He turned to Sister Marie-Bernard's superiors to see what could be done with her.

Finally, turning back to Sister Marie-Bernard, he said, "Perhaps you can help out in the infirmary since I hear you are often sick yourself," dismissing her.

Over the years, Sister Marie-Bernard quietly endured many such events concocted to keep her from becoming proud. The crown of humiliation was often painful. Yet, she was consoled as she prayed the prayer she had once prayed with the exquisite Mother of God. The Lady had smiled at Bernadette and said, "I do not promise to make you happy in this world, but in the next."

The Virgin came to meet her on April 16, 1879, when the thirty-five-year-old Sister Marie-Bernard, suffering terribly from tuberculosis, died at Nevers.

Mystery Prayer

Holy God, you saw your divine Son mocked and spat upon. The Kingdom of God that he announced became the subject of a cruel and hideous joke. Jesus, your suffering servant, was taunted and tortured with a painful crown of thorns. Mary, somehow, you felt the pain and humiliation that Jesus was enduring. Your heart was breaking for him. When I am humiliated and diminished, remind me to suffer without bitterness, without the desire for revenge. Let me act and speak in a way that honors the dignity of every person. Amen.

Mystery Intentions

- Those suffering emotional abuse and ridicule.
- Personal patience, humility, and courage.
- Conversion of those who abuse and persecute others.
- Your own intention(s).

——————— *Fourth Sorrowful Mystery* ———————

THE CARRYING OF THE CROSS

Scripture Passage

LUKE 23:26-32

As they led him away they took hold of a certain Simon, a Cyrenian, who was coming in from the country; and after laying the cross on him, they made him carry it behind Jesus. A large crowd of people followed Jesus, including many women who mourned and lamented him. Jesus turned to them and said, "Daughters of Jerusalem, do not weep for me; weep instead for yourselves and for your children, for indeed, the days are coming when people will say, 'Blessed are the barren, the wombs that never bore and the breasts that never nursed.' At that time people will say to the mountains, 'Fall upon us!' and to the hills, 'Cover us!' for if these things are done when the wood is green what will happen when it is dry?" Now two others, both criminals, were led away with him to be executed.

Reflection

It was Roman practice to put a condemned prisoner in the middle of a square formed by four well-armed soldiers. Before they escorted him to the execution site, the prisoner was given the crossbeam on which he would soon be crucified. He carried it on his shoulders, balancing the weight with both arms, and with his head awkwardly bent forward.

All around the empire, brutal and iron-fisted control was a Roman trademark. To make an example of those being executed and to deter future rebellion or challenges to Roman authority, prisoners were paraded by the longest route. A fifth Roman soldier walked ahead of the condemned man with a placard stating his crime for the crowds to see. For Jesus, the sign read: "Jesus of Nazareth, King of the Jews." John's Gospel says that Pilate made sure the sign was written in Hebrew, Latin, and Greek.

The typical crossbeam, scholars say, weighed from fifty to seventy pounds. That weight makes sense of the report in the three Synoptic Gospels that the Roman soldiers escorting Jesus soon realized that he would not be able to carry his own crossbeam. They pulled a man from the crowd to walk behind the prisoner, carrying the crossbeam on his own shoulders. It is tradition — not Scripture — that suggests that the weakened Jesus staggered and fell several times while carrying the crossbeam. It may be that these falls prompted soldiers to force Simon into service.

Simon was, the Gospels say, from Cyrene (modern-day Shahhat) in Libya. He may have been a Jew, visiting the Holy City for the Passover. The Gospel of Mark further adds that this Simon of Cyrene was "the father of Alexander and Rufus" (Mark 15:21). Although there is no way to verify the connection, some Scripture scholars add that this man could have been the father of the Rufus who was later well known to the Christian community of Rome. Near the end of his epistle to the Romans, St. Paul sent greetings to many in that community, including Rufus, whom he called "chosen in the Lord" (Romans 16:13).

Down through Christian history, Simon of Cyrene has become a more important figure — but in a symbolic way. Simon helped Jesus to carry his heavy cross. For centuries, Christians have been told that they must imitate Simon, and that they, too, must carry crosses, or burdens, for the love of Christ. They should try to follow in the Lord's footsteps, accepting the Father's will and participating in the redemptive suffering of Christ. A great parade of Christian saints — men and women alike — have understood that important invitation to carry Jesus' cross:

- The great St. Francis of Assisi, the thirteenth-century founder of the Order of Friars Minor, told his brothers, "Offer your bodies and take up His holy cross and follow His most holy commands even to the end."
- "You must accept your cross," explained the simple but holy nineteenth-century French parish priest St. John Vianney. "If you bear it courageously it will carry you to Heaven."
- "I understood the cross as the destiny of God's people," wrote St. Teresa Benedicta of the Cross (Edith Stein), a Jewish-born Carmelite martyred in 1942 at Auschwitz. "I felt that those who understood the Cross of Christ should take it upon themselves on everybody's behalf."

Those who follow Jesus see that he didn't reject his cross. In his footsteps and in his memory, Christians shoulder their own.

The Rosary in Our Lives

A Pope's Cross

For at least a decade, Pope John Paul II (1920-2005) continued to serve the world's 1.5 billion Catholics while suffering from Parkinson's disease. As the disease progressed, the pope's speech became slurred, although his mental faculties remained sharp. His hands shook, and he couldn't walk or hold his head erect for more than a few minutes. Near the end of his life, he was in almost constant pain.

In 1998, seven years before the pope's death, Cardinal Joseph Ratzinger, the future Pope Benedict XVI, said of John Paul: "The pain is written on his face. His figure is bent, and he needs to support himself on his pastoral staff. He leans on the cross, on the crucifix. . . ."

Perhaps the Holy Father considered and even discussed resigning from the papacy, although it would have been unprecedented. Instead, he seemed to sense that Jesus was asking him to carry the cross until the end. It was a very heavy cross for a man who lived into his seventies, and then into his eighties.

Some of the burdens the pope shouldered came not from illness but from the great spiritual weight of his office. To be the modern "Vicar of Christ," "Successor of St. Peter," "Supreme Pontiff of the Universal Church," and "Bishop of Rome" implies enormous responsibility and work.

The sex-abuse crisis in the Church stunned and deeply wounded John Paul. An increasing secularization throughout Europe and much of the Western world disturbed him greatly. He warned developed nations that failing to offer protection and respect for all human life would slowly lead them toward a "culture of death."

It also must have been very difficult for the Holy Father when many people inside and outside of the Church began to point fingers at his deteriorating body. Some were embarrassed by what he could no longer do and be. As a young man, and even into his forties and fifties, Karol Wojtyla had been athletic. He was a skilled skier and swimmer who loved soccer, canoeing, mountain climbing, and hiking. When many people would have hidden or downplayed a degenerative illness, the pope wrote and spoke about it often.

Christ does not really tell us why we suffer, the pope admitted in *Salvifici Doloris* (on the Christian meaning of suffering), an apostolic letter written fairly early in his papacy. Instead, Christ beckons us to follow him, to accept our crosses and take up our own crosses. "Gradually," he explained, "*as the individual takes up his cross*, spiritually uniting himself to the Cross of Christ, the salvific meaning of suffering is revealed before him" (n. 26, emphasis in original).

The whole world seemed to respect and honor John Paul's courage during his last days in the spring of 2005. A few days before his death on April 2, 2005, the pope was discharged for the last time from Gemilli Hospital in Rome. He wanted to die in the papal apartments, his home at the Vatican for twenty-six years. His personal "way of the cross" was ending. The last words of Pope John Paul, whispered in Polish, remind us of those of the dying Jesus: "Let me go to the house of the Father."

Mystery Prayer

God, your beloved Son was forced to carry the crossbeam on which he would be nailed. Jesus was "like a lamb led to slaughter / or a sheep silent before shearers, / he did not open his mouth" (Isaiah 53:7). Mary, another sword of grief pierced your heart when you saw your beautiful and loving son stumbling on his "Way of the Cross." Pray for me when I am asked to shoulder a cross and make my way to suffering, and maybe to death. Amen.

Mystery Intentions

· Growing love of Jesus, our Redeemer.
· Strength to carry God-given crosses.
· Help for those who are burdened.
· Your own intention(s).

——————— *Fifth Sorrowful Mystery* ———————

THE CRUCIFIXION

Scripture Passage

JOHN 19:25-30

Standing by the cross of Jesus were his mother and his mother's sister, Mary the wife of Clopas, and Mary of Magdala. When Jesus saw his mother and the disciple there whom he loved, he said to his mother, "Woman, behold, your son." Then he said to the disciple, "Behold, your mother." And from that hour the disciple took her into his home.

After this, aware that everything was now finished, in order that the scripture might be fulfilled, Jesus said, "I thirst." There was a vessel filled with common wine. So they put a sponge soaked in wine on a sprig of hyssop and put it up to his mouth. When Jesus had taken the wine, he said, "It is finished." And bowing his head, he handed over the spirit.

Reflection

Only John's Gospel states that Mary was standing near the cross on Golgotha while her son was dying an excruciating death. Though every part of his body must have been throbbing with pain, the exhausted Jesus thought of his grieving mother. In Jewish society, women without husbands or sons were legally and socially vulnerable. Their status was only slightly more respectable than that of slaves. Jesus wanted to make sure that his beloved mother would be cared for. More than sixty years after that world-changing event on the rocky hill outside of Jerusalem's walls, John, the elderly evangelist, told the story.

Shortly before his death, Jesus — the "Word of God" and "the Father's only Son" — was taking care of others. With just a few words, he provided for his mother and showed his loving trust in John. "Woman, behold, your son," he said to his mother. "Behold, your mother," he said, grimacing with pain and nodding to John.

Theologians maintain that when Jesus gave the care of his mother to John, he was also giving his mother to the community of his followers, and ultimately to his Church. The development of Church teaching about Mary took centuries. But gradually, the Church understood — and taught — that Mary is the Mother of the Church. But the followers of Jesus had honored Mary in a special way almost from the first Christian centuries.

As a victim of crucifixion, Jesus died relatively quickly — within six hours, according to Mark's Gospel. Crucified men sometimes took days to die. The extremely brutal scourging Jesus received undoubtedly drained his strength and mercifully shortened his agony.

Crucifixion killed victims for a variety of reasons, medical authorities explain. Extensive blood loss from crucifixion led to hypovolemic shock. Hypovolemic shock is the inability of the heart to pump because there's no longer enough blood and fluid left for the heart to pump. Slow asphyxiation also occurred because the chest muscles and lungs were hyper-expanded. Eventually, the crucified man could scarcely raise his body enough to inhale. Then, death came quickly, as it apparently did for Jesus.

In the first Christian centuries, the cross was not used as a symbol for those who followed Jesus. The cross reminded them too much of Christ's horrendous death. It was too terrible, too shameful, and too painful. Crucifixion had been used for rebels, traitors, and slaves. Struggling with the fact that Jesus died as a criminal, Christians focused instead on the Resurrection, which followed their Master's death.

Instead of a cross, a simple, stylized fish often represented early Christianity. The Greek word for fish — *ichthys* — gave Christians a secret acrostic. Each letter of the word *ichthys* stood for one word of a simple statement of faith about Jesus: "Jesus Christ, God's Son, [is our] Savior."

In A.D. 341, out of reverence for Jesus, Emperor Constantine, the first Christian Roman emperor, outlawed crucifixion. According to Catholic tradition, Constantine's mother, St. Helena, discovered relics of the true cross of Jesus in Jerusalem, early in the fourth century. After that, Christians began to embrace the cross as a beloved symbol for their Savior and his sacrifice.

The Rosary in Our Lives

BEARING THE WOUNDS OF JESUS

Throughout the hot summer weeks of 1959, seventy-two-year-old Padre Pio Forgione (1887-1968) of Pietrelcina, Italy, was in bed, suffering from a painful cancerous tumor. Over the years, the holiness and spiritual gifts of this priest had drawn hundreds of thousands of visitors. They flocked to visit him at San Giovanni Rotondo Monastery in the Foggia province in southern Italy. For so many years, the priest had spent nineteen-hour days, hearing confessions, meeting visitors, handling correspondence, and praying before the Blessed Sacrament.

Now, however, this gravely ill priest could do little more than move his head to see the image of Our Lady Liberatrix (Our Lady of Liberty) that hung on the wall of his monastery cell. This image of Mary had come from his childhood home in the little village of Pietrelcina.

Padre Pio was suffering his own crucifixion. He was wracked with pain from the cancer spreading quickly through his abdomen. It was a pain he accepted gladly. However, Padre Pio also suffered each day as Jesus did.

In 1910, more than forty years earlier, he had received the stigmata, the wounds of Christ, in his hands, feet, and side. It happened a month after the twenty-three-year-old was ordained a priest. Jesus and Mary appeared to him, and he was given the wounds that other great mystics, including St. Francis of Assisi, had received. The young priest had prayed then that the wounds would remain in his body but invisibly. Pio did not wish to become the center of misguided attention and veneration. For a while, his prayers were answered. The wounds became invisible. But, in 1918, eight years after he first received the wounds, Christ appeared to him again. The visible stigmata returned.

Padre Pio was happy that he might be dying soon. He would see the Lord, whom he loved so well, and the Mother of the Lord, to whom he was completely devoted. He referred to the Blessed Mother as the "beautiful Virgin Mary." Often, however, he just called her "Mother." She was, he said, the "Mediatrix of all graces." She loved her children with a mother's extravagance. "She treats me," he wrote, "as if I were her only child on the face of the earth." For this reason, he maintained, the Rosary was the perfect prayer of intercession to God.

As the scorching days of July passed, the old priest prayed the Rosary constantly in his sickbed. There was nothing new about the way he prayed one Rosary after another. For years, people had noticed that the saintly Padre Pio nearly always had his right hand tucked into the breast pocket of his habit. Although he said nothing to others about this practice, he prayed nonstop with a small chaplet of beads. As a very young seminarian, he decided that he would try not to waste a single second of his life without raising his heart and mind to God.

During the summer weeks that Padre Pio was getting closer to death, the Pilgrim Statue of Our Lady of Fátima was touring Italy. Padre Pio had always had a special love for Our Lady of Fátima and her messages. On August 6, the statue was brought to San Giovanni Rotondo, just for him.

Padre Pio was able to get out of bed and pray before the statue. Later, he heard the helicopter, which was carrying the statue, take off. The statue was heading to the next pilgrimage destination. Suddenly, he prayed aloud: "O Mother of mine, when you came to Italy, you found me with this sickness. You came to visit me here in San Giovanni and found me still suffering from it. Now you are leaving, and I am not delivered from my illness!"

Witnesses in Padre Pio's cell report that a miracle took place as he voiced that prayer. He was asking the Blessed Mother, his Mother, for a healing. The helicopter pilot circled the monastery three times. Padre Pio felt something like lightning shoot through his body. He felt this mysterious "bolt" collide with his tumor. He then felt a surge of heat. The tumor was vaporized, and the miserable pain started melting away. He knew what had happened. "I am healed!" he cried joyfully. "Our Lady has healed me!"

Padre Pio of Pietrelcina had nine more full years of life. With the wounds of Jesus still visible on his body, he died on September 23, 1968. Padre Pio was canonized as a saint thirty-four years later on June 16, 2002.

Mystery Prayer

Father, finally your Son didn't have the strength to take another breath. He surrendered his spirit to you, and died. The bruised and bloody body of Jesus testified to the greatest sacrifice imaginable. Your sinless Son, our Savior, was executed like a common criminal. Mary, when you witnessed your son's death, you must have wished for your own. Yet, you bowed to the Father's will. Strengthen me when I am on the way to God. "Pray for us sinners, now and at the hour of our death." Amen.

Mystery Intentions
- An end to capital punishment.
- A blessed, peaceful death for the dying.
- Conversion of those supporting or considering euthanasia.
- Your own intention(s).

4. THE GLORIOUS MYSTERIES

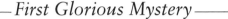 *First Glorious Mystery*

THE RESURRECTION

Scripture Passage

MATTHEW 28:1-7

After the sabbath, as the first day of the week was dawning, Mary Magdalene and the other Mary came to see the tomb. And behold, there was a great earthquake; for an angel of the Lord descended from heaven, approached, rolled back the stone, and sat upon it. His appearance was like lightning and his clothing was white as snow. The guards were shaken with fear of him and became like dead men. Then the angel said to the women in reply, "Do not be afraid! I know that you are seeking Jesus the crucified. He is not here, for he has been raised just as he said. Come and see the place where he lay. Then go quickly and tell his disciples, 'He has been raised from the dead, and he is going before you to Galilee; there you will see him.' Behold, I have told you."

Reflection

An angel, appearing "like lightning," sat on the rock. It was the gigantic rock that had sealed the tomb where the battered and lifeless body of Jesus had been laid three days earlier. To say that Mary Magdalene and the "other Mary" were speechless and stunned is to state the obvious. What went through the minds of these two women? How fast their hearts must have been beating when they encountered the incredibly beautiful and glowing being who was speaking to them about Jesus!

This angel brought the best news ever shared on earth. "Do not be afraid! I know that you are seeking Jesus the crucified. He is not here, for he has been raised just as he said." Then the angel invited the two Marys to see for themselves. The body of Jesus was no longer in the tomb. He told them to go quickly and tell the others about the Resurrection of Jesus. And so the resurrection news spread to the disciples, to the other followers of Jesus, and to the world.

Twenty centuries later, the Resurrection of Christ is still the most important news we can share. Christ's resurrection confirms all of his works and teachings. The truth of Jesus' divinity is verified by his rising from the dead. Without the Resurrection, Christianity is simply a wonderful fairy tale, an edifying story. If Jesus didn't rise from the dead, he was simply a good man, an inspiring prophet.

If Christ didn't rise from the dead, added St. Paul, "then empty [too] is our preaching; empty, too, your faith" (1 Corinthians 15:14). Paul, "the thirteenth apostle," and the theologian of the New Testament, was a realist. He could see that the Resurrection confirmed everything that Jesus said and did. In our own day, the Church couldn't agree more. "The Resurrection of Jesus," states the *Catechism of the Catholic Church*, "is the crowning truth of our faith in Christ" (CCC 638).

In all four Gospels, appearances of the resurrected Jesus are told with great detail. In all, scholars say, more than five hundred people later saw the risen Lord and testified that he had truly conquered death. So many people in such different circumstances and locations could not have been duped. A massive plot to deceive the world could not have lasted long.

Even the Jews who had engineered Christ's conviction couldn't explain how armed Roman guards had allowed the unarmed followers of Jesus to steal his body. The soldiers denied falling asleep and had been given strict orders to stay alert. Moving the stone that had sealed the tomb of Jesus would have taken many strong men to accomplish. It would have been a noisy operation.

Matthew's Gospel says that some of the guards soon went to the chief priests and reported that the tomb had been opened and that the body of Jesus had mysteriously disappeared. They had no idea how it had happened. The priests, according to this evangelist, paid the guards well to say that the disciples had stolen the body while they slept.

Such plots and lies could not hide the glorious truth. Jesus did rise from the dead, confirming his divinity. His resurrection, unlike that of Lazarus and others whom he had raised, was different. He would never return to earthly life as they did. The raised body of Jesus was no longer confined to time and space. He was able to be with his followers whenever he wished. Because he broke the bonds of death, Jesus would forever be much more than a heroic figure, the founder of a church.

Jesus is a presence, a person whom we can know and love deeply. Jesus is alive!

The Rosary in Our Lives

I Also See the Resurrection

Eighty-two-year-old Betty Dolezal, a mother of twelve children, had certainly enjoyed a full life when she learned in early 2002 that she had a cancerous brain tumor. Doctors advised Betty and her husband, Bernard, a general and family-practice physician, that she should undergo surgery in Indianapolis, where the best specialists were available. Treatment to stem the spread of any cancer was to be followed up back home.

Betty was certainly thinking about her life, her family, and the many blessings they had received as she prepared for the surgery. She also knew that death could be coming soon. She was so grateful. Betty was a convert to Catholicism, with a never-ending curiosity and interest in her adopted faith. Even as a busy mom, she was always an avid reader of spiritual literature. With millions of other Catholics from around the world, she had also traveled on pilgrimage to Medjugorje. She wanted to visit the little village in Bosnia and Herzegovina where the Virgin Mary allegedly began appearing to six young people in 1981. The appearances continued every day, many people claimed.

After she came home from Medjugorje, her family noticed that Betty had a much deeper peace and persistence in prayer. Betty started a Friday-morning prayer group for women in her parish. On her own, she rose early every day and came downstairs to the living room, where she had permanently moved a chair to face a large window. From her "prayer chair," Betty watched each new day dawn as she prayed her Rosary and read Scripture.

Better than anyone else, Betty could see that there was plenty of pain in the lives of her eleven surviving children. They had lost a brother — and she had lost a son — to a hit-and-run driver right before his twenty-first birthday. Even more tragic, perhaps, was the friction and anger that developed somehow between several of the kids, some of whom wouldn't even speak to one another.

With the perspective that only many years of faith-filled living can give, Betty saw where the seeds of alienation had been planted in her children. For one thing, she knew that her husband's busy medical practice had been difficult for their children. They resented the way he invested himself so totally in his work. Some of that investment was part of the job description for any doctor in active practice. But, like many men of his generation, this father had been trained to think that raising children was "women's work."

Practically speaking, Betty became the ambassador between her husband and children. She carried messages back and forth between them because there was little or no communication otherwise. In any family with twelve unique boys and girls, lots of support, guidance, time, and love are needed from both parents. Sometimes, Betty could see that her kids simply didn't get what they needed from one or both of their parents.

For a number of years, Betty Dolezal let her children know that she was praying hard for them. Something very precious among them — a loving unity — had died. Betty knew, however, that Jesus is the Lord of all life, the resurrected Christ. She also knew that God is the Father of all families. She continued to ask the Blessed Virgin to intercede for her family. She wanted an "Easter Sunday" for her family.

Right after Betty's surgery, the Dolezal children reunited for the care of their mother. Some of them hadn't seen one another in ten years. A brand-new day began for them. When their mother died of a detached blood clot three months later, in June 2002, the bonds of the Dolezal children tightened even more. They knew their mother wanted them to care for their grieving and ailing father. Bernard died just eleven months after Betty, on the feast of Pentecost, in 2003.

After her parents were gone, one daughter recalled a poignant and prophetic moment with her mother on the day that Betty and Bernard headed to Indianapolis for Betty's brain surgery. Betty was sitting in the living room in her "prayer chair," where she had prayed early morning Rosaries for her family for many years. She gazed out the window reflectively.

"Do you know what I see?" Betty Dolezal whispered to Kathy. "I see the whole passion of Jesus." Then Betty broke into the most joyous grin. "But I also see the Resurrection, and it is so beautiful."

The peaceful grin didn't leave her as she got into the car for the drive to Indianapolis.

Mystery Prayer

Glorious God, your Son, Jesus, conquered death and rose on the third day. The grave could not hold him. Through his sufferings and death, Jesus had redeemed all of your children for all time. Mary, when Jesus rose from the dead, your heart was filled with Resurrection joy. Teach me to see beyond my sufferings and coming death. Help me to renew and share my Resurrection faith each day. Amen.

Mystery Intentions

- New faith in the Resurrection.
- Renewed joy in Christian churches.
- Care for the endangered environment and the Earth.
- Your own intention(s).

———————— *Second Glorious Mystery* ————————

THE ASCENSION

Scripture Passage

LUKE 24:50-53

Then he led them [out] as far as Bethany, raised his hands, and blessed them. As he blessed them he parted from them and was taken up to heaven. They did him homage and then returned to Jerusalem with great joy, and they were continually in the temple praising God.

Reflection

In many ways, we don't know how to celebrate the Ascension of Jesus, which occurs forty days after Easter. It is as wrapped in shining mystery as was the glorious body of Jesus, which lifted off the ground and rose quickly into the sky. He had been standing with his disciples and family. Moments later, his receding figure moved through clouds and slipped through a seam in the bright blue Judean sky. The followers of Jesus knew that Jesus was, and would be, from then on, at the right hand of God the Father. The Ascension of Jesus was, wrote Cardinal John Henry Newman, the "crown of His great work . . . the completion of his redemption . . . for now man is actually in heaven. He has entered into possession of his inheritance."

There was unspeakable joy among those staring up into the sky. They loved Jesus so much. His parting from them was glorious, triumphant. And yet, surely, there was also grief welling up in their hearts. Peter, Andrew, James, John, and the others knew. Mary, the mother of Jesus knew. They knew that they would miss those dark eyes shining with love. The apostles would miss the way Jesus would suddenly throw his strong arm across their backs and shoulders as they walked up and down the hills of Galilee. They knew they would miss hearing him laugh and sing.

In the wonderful economy of God, however, endings are also beginnings. The ending of Christ's earthly life prepared for the birth of the Church. For forty days, Jesus stayed with his disciples. In Jewish tradition, forty was the number of completion, wholeness. The days Jesus spent with his disciples were very full. He ate with them, walked, and talked with them. He helped heal the wounded, humiliated spirit of Peter, who had denied his master three times. Over and over, Jesus reassured these men and women that they would be strengthened and empowered when the Spirit came. They would be equipped to carry on his work, his healing and teaching.

The companions of Jesus couldn't forget what he had said to them: "It is better for you that I go" (John 16:7). Why? Jesus had to return to his Father so that the Holy Spirit could come. The Holy Spirit would then be a presence that dwelt within them. More than once, Jesus had promised, "You will receive power when the Holy Spirit comes upon you" (Acts 1:8).

The disciples also gradually understood that the Ascension was opening heaven to them and to all humanity as well. Jesus had always made it clear that God was "our Father." The same love that the Father had to give His son, Jesus, was available to his other children as well. Like Jesus, our bodies — as well as our spirits — would eventually find a home with God.

Right before he ascended, according to the Acts of the Apostles, Jesus commissioned his disciples: "You will be my witnesses," he said, "to the ends of the earth" (Acts 1:8). Jesus was handing over his ministry to rough and simple fishermen. But he was also prophesying that they would eventually take his message to every corner of the world.

Today, the *Catechism of the Catholic Church* reminds us that the Ascension of Jesus has three important faith lessons about the Kingdom of God (CCC 665-667). First of all, Jesus ascended in his full humanity (body and soul) to sit at his Father's right hand and will one day come back for the Last Judgment. Second, because Jesus, the head of the Church, went before us into heaven, we have reason to hope that we will join him there someday. Third, Jesus can and does intercede for us in heaven, reminding us that the Holy Spirit is constantly renewing and empowering us here on earth.

The Rosary in Our Lives

To the Ends of the World

On a sunny October morning in 1879, the white-haired cardinal rose from a sanctuary chair and walked stiffly to the pulpit. John Henry Newman (1801-1890) smiled broadly at the fresh-faced boys seated in front of him in the chapel at Oscott College. Cardinal Newman had been in this beautiful Gothic church, just north of Birmingham, many times before. In fact, in 1852, he had delivered what came to be known as his "Second Spring" homily from this pulpit. That day, his homily had been given in praise of the re-emergence of Catholicism in Victorian England.

The seventy-eight-year-old Cardinal Newman knew very well that his remarks on this feast of the Holy Rosary had to be short and to the point. He knew schoolboys. He knew all about the way their minds would drift like huge white clouds on a windy day. The cardinal had not written out his homily. He wanted to make sure that he spoke simply and clearly. He planned to speak about the Rosary and then focus on a Gospel text from Luke: "So they went in haste and found Mary and Joseph, and the infant lying in the manger" (Luke 2:16).

The cardinal began his talk by explaining that he had always found it best to pray the Rosary with a mental image or picture for each mystery. "Fix your mind upon that picture of the Annunciation or the Agony in the Garden," he told the boys, "while you say the Pater [Our Father] and the ten Aves [Hail Marys], not thinking of the words, only saying them correctly.

"The Rosary gives us the great truths of Christ's life and death to meditate upon, and brings them nearer to our hearts," he added. "And so we contemplate all the great mysteries of His life and His birth in the manger; and so too the mysteries of His suffering and His glorified life."

"Perhaps this [approach] will overcome any sense of tedium," he said, looking at the fidgeting boys.

Even as he offered these remarks about the Rosary, Cardinal Newman may have been thinking about the way he once viewed the Rosary and all things Catholic. While touring Italy with a friend when he was in his early thirties, years before his conversion, Newman wrote home that Rome was "the most wonderful place on Earth." The Roman Catholic religion, on the other hand, was "polytheistic, degrading and idolatrous."

At forty-four, however, Newman had become a Catholic after almost a decade of intellectual engagement with Catholic theology and history. In the painful months before he was received into the Catholic Church, he often thought of Jesus on the day of his ascension into heaven. It must have been difficult for Christ's apostles to visualize their future without him. But the Lord had assured them, "You will be my witnesses . . . to the ends of the earth" (Acts 1:8). Newman knew that he had to witness to the truth as he had come to see it. His decision to enter the Catholic Church had alienated many of his Anglican friends and members of his family — his own dear family.

"Family!" The cardinal raised his voice a bit, and some of the drifting boys sat up straight. For a moment, they gave their attention again to the most famous churchman in England. The Rosary, he continued, helps us to look at the relationships in the Holy Family, the home in which God lived. "Stay connected with this holy family, with this home where God lived," he advised the boys.

The great cardinal reminded these boys that they would soon grow up and make their way in the world. "Most men who know the world find it a world of great trouble, and disappointments, and even misery," he warned. "If it turns out so to you, seek a home in the Holy Family that you think about in the mysteries of the Rosary."

The elderly cardinal pulled his own black rosary — his "beads" — out of the side pocket of his red cardinal's cassock. He held the rosary high. He knew that he had shared what he could share with these boys. Oscott College was certainly not "the ends of the earth." But Cardinal John Henry Newman hoped that he had witnessed with the heart of an apostle.

On September 19, 2010, Cardinal Newman was beatified by Pope Benedict XVI in England.

Mystery Prayer

Father of us all, after Jesus rose and spent forty precious days with his followers, he ascended to you. As the Son of God, he took his place at your right hand. One day, he will return to judge the living and the dead. Mary, Mother of our Redeemer, you heard Jesus remind his followers, "You will be my witnesses to the ends of the earth." Help me to see how Jesus wants me to witness in his name, today. Amen.

Mystery Intentions

· Mentors and those they mentor.
· Courage and faith when transitions come.
· Accepting Jesus as a teacher and guide.
· Your own intention(s).

--------- *Third Glorious Mystery* ---------

THE DESCENT OF THE HOLY SPIRIT

Scripture Passage

ACTS 2:1-4

When the time for Pentecost was fulfilled, they were all in one place together. And suddenly there came from the sky a noise like a strong driving wind, and it filled the entire house in which they were. Then there appeared to them tongues as of fire, which parted and came to rest on each one of them. And they were all filled with the holy Spirit and began to speak in different tongues, as the Spirit enabled them to proclaim.

Reflection

It's hard to imagine what the Pentecost experience was for the followers of Jesus gathered in Jerusalem. About

120 men and women were waiting in the city for the Spirit, just as Jesus had instructed. They didn't know what would happen, but they did believe that the Spirit would come. They believed it because Jesus had promised it. Jesus said, "But you will receive power when the holy Spirit comes upon you, and you will be my witnesses in Jerusalem, throughout Judea and Samaria, and to the ends of the earth" (Acts 1:8).

Did they nod to one another with a suspicious joy when they heard that strange rushing noise that sounded "like a strong driving wind"? The Acts of the Apostles says the noise came from the sky and filled the house with a rushing, refreshing wind. Likely, it cooled every sweaty face and ruffled every person's clothing and hair.

Surely, James, John, Peter, and all of the other disciples made eye contact with one another. Surely, they whispered reassuring words to those who look alarmed. On the faces of some — including the Mother of the Lord — there must have been a joyful smile. The mysterious wind whistled and whipped its way around them, as though the Spirit of God wanted everyone's attention. This wind was full of power and purpose. As everyone quickly gathered in one room, they began to sense that this wind was also full of love.

The closest friends of Jesus were remembering what he once told the Pharisee Nicodemus. Nicodemus knew every word of the law but could not understand the deeper spiritual truths that Jesus was trying to explain. "The wind blows where it wills, and you can hear the sound it makes, but you do not know where it comes from or where it goes; so it is with everyone born of the Spirit," Jesus had told him (John 3:8).

A peace settled over the closest friends of Jesus, and a magnificent red-orange globe of light appeared in the quiet, dimly lit room. Like small flashes of lightning, flames shot out from the globe. Flames settled above each head. They burned brightly and steadily, washing every face with golden light. Each disciple joyfully scanned the room to see the Spirit's fire gently burning above every brother and sister.

United through fire, each one began to feel a fire burning within. Spontaneously, this new community of the empowered, gifted followers of Jesus burst into song. Their voices soon filled the house as they sang one hymn of praise after another. The tongues of fire that had started above their heads seemed to have rekindled their spirits.

Peter and the others poured out into the street and began to share the Good News with courage, passion, and joy. Jews of every nationality came closer to hear the Galileans, whose faces were now radiant. These ex-fishermen were speaking in dozens of different languages, but the message was the same. Jesus, explained Peter, had been raised up by God, "releasing him from the throes of death" (Acts 2:24). Death couldn't hold the Messiah, Peter explained to astonished Jews, who found themselves convinced by everything he said.

The disciples moved courageously into the gathering crowds. Despite the threats of the Jews and the Romans, the fire of Pentecost couldn't be quenched. A newborn passion to spread the Gospel couldn't be held back. The Church had been born out of wind and fire. The followers of Jesus were taking up his work.

The Rosary in Our Lives

THE GIFT OF COURAGE

Fifty-nine-year-old Dona Amelia Bastos had not planned to listen in on the men at her house in Rio de Janeiro in 1962. Her husband, a retired army doctor, and his friends argued late into that hot June night about the best ways to stop a communist takeover in their beloved nation.

Though it was incredibly rich with untapped natural resources, Brazil was suffering from spiraling inflation and unrest. The Brazilian president, João Goulart, had been assigning many high-level government positions to communists or those sympathetic to communism. Ammunition was being smuggled into the country to arm guerrilla teams being secretly trained for a communist-inspired overthrow of the government. Pamphlets with Marxist propaganda were being used to teach illiterate people to read. U.S. Attorney General Robert F. Kennedy had traveled to Brazil to meet President Goulart and share President Kennedy's concern about Brazil's economic chaos and the potential for revolution.

Dona Amelia knew that businessmen and professionals like her husband had been organizing politically for several years. They formed organizations to study what was really happening politically, economically, and culturally. They pooled resources to publish pamphlets warning the public about freedoms that Brazilians could lose. Just look at what happened in Hungary, East Germany, Poland, and more recently in Cuba, the pamphlets said.

Dona Amelia, a former teacher, was a petite, dynamic, and natural leader. She was also a deeply committed Catholic. The day after that worrisome gathering of her husband's friends, she invited some women to her house. She couldn't resist getting involved and inviting other Brazilian women to do the same. "I suddenly decided," she told her friends, "that politics had become too important to be left entirely to the men." Everyone laughed but could also see that she meant it.

Dona Amelia believed that organized women and the power of prayer could be Brazil's salvation from communism. With thirty other housewives and mothers, she soon formed CAMDE, the Campaign of Women for Democracy.

CAMDE certainly had political goals, but the women of Brazil understood that they were being empowered for reasons that went way beyond politics. Rosary crusades led by Father Patrick Peyton from the United States inspired many Brazilians in 1962 and 1963.

The women organized quickly and began to produce and distribute pamphlets about the dangers of communism. They urged everyone to pray the Rosary for Brazil's future. Like the disciples in Jerusalem at Pentecost, the women rejoiced at the gifts God was giving them. They felt ready to share the truth, with power and courage. Like Peter and the other apostles who rushed out into Jerusalem's streets to share the Good News, they were being heard and welcomed everywhere.

In Belo Horizonte, twenty thousand women marched together, reciting the Rosary aloud. Their peaceful demonstration broke up the leftist meeting there. When President Goulart appointed a leftist prime minister, several dozen CAMDE women went together to Rio de Janeiro's newspapers. They wanted the papers to publicize their objections to the appointment. Newspaper editors shrugged and admitted that the women would have to show their strength in numbers. Dona Amelia and her friends understood and prayed.

On March 13, 1964, however, President Goulart decided that the time had come for a coup. With government funds, he had a hundred thousand communist activists from all over Brazil transported into Rio. On television, the president announced that massive changes were needed. The Communist Party should be legalized, he said, and privately owned oil refineries and large land tracts should be handed over for government control and redistribution. The Congress was to be abolished in favor of assemblies comprised of workers, peasants, and soldiers.

Brazilians could see that their president was trying to incite civil war — and a communist takeover. On March 19, the "March of the Family With God Toward Freedom" answered President Goulart. Dona Amelia Bastos and six hundred thousand women courageously marched through São Paulo. Some were carrying prayer books and rosaries; others were wearing rosaries around their necks. They also distributed a thirteen-hundred-word proclamation. It began with the statement, "This nation which God has given us, immense and marvelous as it is, is in extreme danger."

"Mother of God," the proclamation continued, "preserve us from the fate and suffering of the martyred women of Cuba, Poland, Hungary, and other enslaved nations!"

The women's public witness and prayer fed the resistance to communism, which had been spreading throughout Brazil — like Pentecostal fire. On April 1, 1964, President Goulart fled Brazil for Paraguay.

Mystery Prayer

Holy Spirit, you came with a rush of wind and fire upon the disciples of Jesus in Jerusalem. You filled them with wonderful gifts and charisms to continue the Kingdom work of Jesus. Mary, you, too, knew the mighty but sweet power of the Spirit. Open my eyes and heart to recognize and use the gifts I have. They come from the Holy Spirit. I am part of Pentecost. Amen.

Mystery Intentions

· Faith in the Holy Spirit.
· Renewal and new fire in the Church.
· Using our gifts to build the Kingdom of God.
· Your own intention(s).

Fourth Glorious Mystery

THE ASSUMPTION

Scripture Passage

1 CORINTHIANS 15:54-55

And when this which is corruptible clothes itself with incorruptibility and this which is mortal clothes itself with immortality, then the word that is written shall come about:

> "Death is swallowed up in victory.
> Where, O death, is your victory?
> Where, O death, is your sting?"

Reflection

"Good news travels fast," reports the old adage. That was certainly true in Jerusalem when the apostles — one tradition suggests that it was Thomas — discovered that the tomb of Mary, the Mother of Jesus, was empty. The apostles and the newborn Church were overjoyed, but probably not surprised. Although the doctrine about Mary's "immaculate conception" would not be formally defined for more than eighteen hundred years, it was understood in the early Church that Mary was holy in a totally new way. Therefore, the proper place for Mary — body and soul — was in heaven. The followers of Jesus believed that she was fully assumed, or taken up, into heaven.

In fact, the Assumption was the first Marian feast to be celebrated by Christians. After Constantine became the first Christian emperor in the fourth century, the feast was called simply the "Memory of Mary." Initially, it was celebrated only in Palestine but later throughout the Eastern Church as well. In the seventh century, the devotion began to be celebrated in Rome and the Western Church.

It was called the "Falling Asleep," or the Dormition, of the Mother of God. Gradually, the Church began to call it the Assumption, since the teaching involved much more than the end of Mary's life on earth. The feast also celebrated Mary's unique identity and role in redemption history. An angel had addressed her as "favored one," assuring her that "the Lord is with you" (Luke 1:28). Mary then became the Mother of the Son of God.

Nonetheless, the teaching about Mary's assumption into heaven was not universally embraced. Some Christians apparently had never heard of it. In 451, during the Council of Chalcedon in Constantinople, the emperor Marcian asked if the "relics" of Mary could be brought from Jerusalem to Constantinople, since it was then the capital of the Eastern Roman Empire.

The patriarch of Jerusalem must have been surprised by the question. He patiently explained that there were no relics of Mary at all. She died in the presence of the apostles, he said, but her tomb was later found empty. The apostles, the patriarch continued, concluded that Mary's body, reunited with her spirit, was taken to heaven to be with her son, Jesus.

Throughout most of the nineteen centuries after her life on earth, the development of this teaching about Mary seemed to develop very slowly. The dogma of Mary's assumption was only formally declared by Pope Pius XII in 1950. The actual proclamation was brief: "The Immaculate Mother of God, the ever Virgin Mary, having completed the course of her earthly life, was assumed body and soul into heaven."

The Church understood that any celebration of Mary's life should be grounded in the way she participated in the redemptive work of her son, Jesus. The central mystery of her life and person was the fact that she became the mother of God's Son.

Because of this blessed identity, the Church reasoned in reverse. God would not have wanted the body of his Son's mother to decay, as do the bodies of other human beings. Although Jesus ascended body and soul into heaven because of his own divine power, God raised "Holy Mary" into paradise to live eternally with her son, Jesus.

The Church also draws another lesson from Mary's assumption. This feast, celebrated on August 15 around the world, reminds us that we, too, can follow Mary into glory when our lives are over. There will be a day for the resurrection of our bodies. The Assumption is a feast of hope for all humanity.

The Rosary in Our Lives

LISTEN TO YOUR MOTHER

When David Cavillo's mother, Alicia, died in 2010, following a long illness, he knew he had two attentive, loving, and devoted mothers in heaven. He was really happy that his earthly mother had lived to see how he had changed. It was she who had promoted the seeds of change — or the "beads of change" — many years earlier.

By 2008, David, a forty-seven-year-old highly successful attorney in McAllen, Texas, had come to a low point in his marriage and in his life. The stresses of running a successful law practice had collided with the responsibilities and demands of being a husband and father of five children. Friends and family members urged him to attend an ACTS (Adoration, Community, Theology, and Service) retreat for men.

David remembers sitting in his minivan in the monastery parking lot where the retreat was about to begin. Very stressed, he was shaking and trying to decide whether or not he would go in. When his brother and teenage son,

David, Jr., drove up to wish him well, he decided he had to attend the retreat. No way out.

In the course of the weekend, David felt a new peace settling into his spirit, and during the retreat, he prayed the Rosary with seventy-nine other men. He was totally surprised by his reaction to the experience. Meditating on the mysteries of salvation, and hearing men's voices reciting the Our Father and the Hail Mary, profoundly moved this articulate and savvy litigator.

"I felt this amazing connection," David explained. "I felt that I was praying with God himself, and with everybody who had ever prayed the Rosary. I felt that I was praying with my mom!" The experience, he laughed, was certainly "the Holy Spirit slapping me upside the head."

David remembered the advice his mother had been offering since his childhood: "Pray the Rosary; put the Rosary at the center of your prayer life." Throughout adolescence and adulthood, David Cavillo had ignored his mother's advice. "It wasn't cool enough for me, and I was too macho to be praying the Rosary," he confessed.

Like so many other men, David had assumed that the Rosary devotion was for "old ladies and funerals." Stating that misconception — as if it were factual — is the way he now opens talks about the Rosary. People laugh — especially men. From then on, however, they listen more carefully. With his wife, Valerie, David founded an Internet site, "Real Men Pray the Rosary," which features a busy Facebook page. The Cavillos were very pleased to see that more than half the Facebook "friends" were men under the age of thirty-five.

David has read everything he could find about the Rosary but believes that Pope John Paul II's 2002 apostolic letter *Rosarium Virginis Mariae* ("The Rosary of the Virgin Mary") is a great treasure for a world hungering to learn or relearn how to pray. The mission statement for Real Men Pray the Rosary is taken directly from the pope's letter, he said. RMPTR's mission is to promote the Rosary "with conviction, in the light of Scripture, in harmony with the liturgy, and in the context of our daily lives."

The Rosary now plays a role in the daily life of the Cavillo family. David and Valerie are teaching their six children the prayer practice and how to meditate on the Rosary mysteries, which recap the life of Jesus and his Blessed Mother. David has also urged other Catholic lawyers to pick up and pray the Rosary.

David told colleagues that lawyers are inevitably "dipped" every day into a culture of deception, fraud, mistrust, and violence. Spending twenty-five or thirty minutes with Jesus and Mary while praying the Rosary can help spiritually lift lawyers above the ugly milieu in which they often work.

Mystery Prayer

Creator God, when you created the mother of your Son in her mother's womb, you set her free from the stain of sin. Immaculately conceived, she said yes to the plan you had for her and the sinful world. After the end of her earthly life, Jesus called her to heaven, body and soul, so that corruption would never touch her. Mary, I rejoice in your assumption. Remind me each day, that I — and all the children of God — can have that same destiny. Amen.

Mystery Intentions
- Those afraid of death.
- Honor for Mary as the Mother of God's Son.
- Faith in the resurrection of the body.
- Your own intention(s).

—————— *The Fifth Glorious Mystery* ——————

THE CROWNING OF OUR LADY QUEEN OF HEAVEN

Scripture Passage
REVELATION 12:1-5

A great sign appeared in the sky, a woman clothed with the sun, with the moon under her feet, and on her head a crown of twelve stars. She was with child and wailed aloud in pain as she labored to give birth. Then another sign appeared in the sky; it was a huge red dragon, with seven heads and ten horns, and on its heads were seven diadems. Its tail swept away a third of the stars in the sky and hurled them down to the earth. Then the dragon stood before the woman about to give birth, to devour her child when she gave birth. She gave birth to a son, a male child, destined to rule all the nations with an iron rod. Her child was caught up to God and his throne.

Reflection

Mary, the Mother of Jesus, probably never saw herself as the "Queen of heaven," a title formally given to her by the Catholic Church and celebrated often in religious art. Rather, Mary may have described herself as she did to the angel Gabriel, when the angel asked this teenage girl to become the mother of God's Son.

"Behold, I am the handmaid of the Lord," she answered. "May it be done to me according to your word" (Luke 1:38). Mary was humble, little, devoted, prayerful, and obedient. She said yes to God, accepting whatever God would ask, even when she didn't fully understand what that yes would mean.

Marian titles and imagery have grown as Marian theology developed through the centuries. The followers of Jesus, it seems, loved to honor his Blessed Mother. For centuries, the Church has agreed that devotion to Mary is very fitting.

In 431, at the Council of Ephesus, Mary was given the Greek title *Theotokos*, or "God-bearer." In the Western Church, this title was translated as "the Mother of God." So, the honor and devotion that Mary receives is due to her status as the Mother of Jesus, the Son of God and our Savior.

The title "Queen of heaven" also has rich scriptural roots, scholars remind us. In Luke's Gospel, the angel Gabriel assures Mary that Jesus would be a king. "He will be great and will be called Son of the Most High, and the Lord God will give him the throne of David his father, and he will rule over the house of Jacob forever, and of his kingdom there will be no end" (Luke 1:32-33). Because Jesus is a king, Mary was seen as the mother of a king and as "Queen Mother."

For centuries, Mary has been depicted in sacred art as a queen, reigning gloriously in heaven. The title "Queen" was also given to her in the Litany of Loreto, an ancient prayer that may have originated in the early Middle Ages. The litany was approved for public use by Pope Sixtus V in 1587. The prayer appeals for Mary's help under her titles of "Queen of angels," "Queen of patriarchs," "Queen of prophets," "Queen of apostles," "Queen of martyrs," "Queen of confessors," "Queen of virgins," "Queen of all saints," "Queen conceived without original sin," "Queen assumed into heaven," "Queen of the holy Rosary," "Queen of families," and "Queen of peace."

In 1954, Pope Pius XII released the encyclical *Ad Caeli Reginam* (on proclaiming the Queenship of Mary). In that encyclical, the pope also established the feast of the Queenship of Mary on May 31. That was the last day of May, the month traditionally dedicated to Marian devotions. In 1969, however, Pope Paul VI moved the date to August 22, one week after the celebration of her assumption.

Each pope, it seems, has encouraged and built upon the devotion that gives Mary the honor she is due. At the

Angelus gathering on the feast of Christ the King in 2006, Pope Benedict XVI told the crowd that the cross of Christ was actually the "throne" on which Jesus showed the world the glorious "God-love." But the pope also said that Mary, the Mother of Jesus, should be our model because she accepted God's will in her life with humility and absolute faith. That acceptance of God's will in her life, the pope said, was the reason that "God exalted her over all other creatures, and Christ crowned her Queen of heaven and earth."

It also seems, however, that Mary has been unofficially crowned in our hearts for many generations. Many Catholic nations, such as Portugal and Poland, named Mary as their spiritual Queen, asking for her special protection. The May Crowning devotion, a popular practice in the United States and in many other countries in Europe, is another example of a popular acknowledgment of Mary's queenship. A procession and the singing of Marian hymns are followed by the crowning of a statue of Mary. Mary is crowned with — and inevitably smiles upon — each simple wreath of flowers.

The Rosary in Our Lives

CHERISHING HUMAN LIFE

As a military chaplain earlier in his priesthood, Cardinal John J. O'Connor of New York (1920-2000) had often seen the human agonies of war. During the Vietnam War in the late 1960s, he frequently gave dying soldiers the last rites. He comforted them, held their hands, assured them of God's mercy, and heard their confessions.

Years later, in the 1980s, the newly appointed archbishop of New York touched the tragic result of human hatred and violence once again. While visiting the former Nazi concentration camp of Dachau, in Germany, he looked into the brick crematorium oven and envisioned the intermixed ashes of Jews and Christians, who had been exterminated many years earlier in the Holocaust. Although he certainly knew about the Holocaust, that experience deeply chilled and horrified him. These innocent people hadn't had anyone to comfort them or hold their hands in the last moments of life.

"Good God," he said, whenever he talked about Dachau, "how could human beings do this to other human beings?"

Back in the United States, Cardinal O'Connor sensed that the Mother of God would help him find new ways to protect all human life and build reverence for it. He had a lifelong devotion to Mary and to the Rosary as a prayer of intercession. "I'm a 'Hail Mary' man," he often quipped when asked about his prayer life. The cardinal would display his best deadpan face, but everyone realized that he wasn't really kidding.

From his boyhood, Cardinal O'Connor had prayed the Rosary daily. He started his day with the Rosary, meditating carefully and thoughtfully on its mysteries. The cardinal drew great inspiration for his enormously demanding job in the Church from the Scripture-based lessons that the Rosary mysteries proclaimed.

Though Mary's glorious status as Queen of heaven fascinated him, Cardinal O'Connor often told others that he was struck by Mary's beginnings. She was just a simple teenage girl in Nazareth when she agreed to surrender her will to God. Because she made herself the handmaid of the Lord so completely, God crowned her. God raised her into heavenly glory, where all the saints and angels now honor her as Queen.

That Marian model of surrendering to God made more sense to him, Cardinal O'Connor said, when he reflected on advice given to him in 1979 by Mother Teresa of Calcutta. Right after he was ordained as a bishop in Rome, she counseled the future cardinal to "Give God permission. . . ." When he thought about she meant by "permission," he realized that she was saying that nothing should be held back from God. The road to each one's personal crown of glory begins with that complete surrender. That understanding shaped his ministry from then on.

In 1990, in the diocesan paper, *Catholic New York*, the cardinal wrote a column titled "Help Wanted: Sisters of Life." Cardinal O'Connor wanted to see a brand-new religious order of women founded. These sisters would minister to needy pregnant women, mothers, and their children. Their mission would also include pro-life education and prayer, including Eucharistic Adoration and the Rosary.

The cardinal's "want ad" hit the mark immediately. In fact, the response was almost unbelievable. There were plenty of Catholic women — in the archdiocese of New York and beyond — who wanted to devote themselves to a real-life, practical, pro-life ministry. That's what the cardinal had in mind. Within a year, the Sisters of Life congregation was already forming, with eight dedicated women as its first members. Within less than twenty years, the congregation of sisters, founded by a cardinal's determination to defend human life, had grown to over sixty members.

Throughout his years shepherding and serving one of the largest dioceses in the United States, Cardinal O'Connor continued to "give God permission" in his life. It was the key, he believed, to letting God accomplish great things through us, just as God did through Mary. In 1999, he was diagnosed with a cancerous brain tumor. He died at the chancery on May 3, 2000, rosary in hand. He was still serving as the archbishop of New York.

Mystery Prayer
Almighty God, you knew that Mary was beyond compare among your creatures. We agree and give her count-

less titles. She is "Seat of wisdom," "Mirror of justice," "Mystical rose," "House of gold," "Morning star," "Gate of heaven," "Ark of the covenant," and much, much more. In heaven, you made her Queen. Mary, here on earth, you are also our gentle, loving queen. Today, as I go about my day, please guide me. Show me how to serve the Kingdom of God here on earth. Amen.

Mystery Intentions
- Understanding of Mary's role in salvation.
- Support for rightful authority.
- Honor for Mary in all Christian churches.
- Your own intention(s).

AS YOU PRAY: A HANDS-ON GUIDE TO THE ROSARY

OVERVIEW OF THE ROSARY

The Rosary is always prayed with the Sign of the Cross, the Apostles' Creed, the Our Father, the Hail Mary, and the Glory Be. Some who pray it add the Fátima Prayer following the Glory Be, which concludes each decade of the Rosary. Others pray the Hail Holy Queen after the full Rosary is prayed. (See the text and sequence for those prayers below.)

With the 2002 addition of the Mysteries of Light (Luminous Mysteries), suggested by Pope John Paul II in his apostolic letter *Rosarium Virginis Mariae* ("The Rosary of the Virgin Mary"), the weekly schedule for praying the mysteries changed from the one that had been observed for many centuries. Now the schedule for the four sets of mysteries is the following:

The Rosary Mystery Schedule

SUNDAY: The Glorious Mysteries
MONDAY: The Joyful Mysteries
TUESDAY: The Sorrowful Mysteries
WEDNESDAY: The Glorious Mysteries
THURSDAY: The Luminous Mysteries
FRIDAY: The Sorrowful Mysteries
SATURDAY: The Joyful Mysteries

USING THE MYSTERIES TO MEDITATE

Although praying with the Luminous Mysteries is optional, most people believe that they greatly enrich the practice of the Rosary. These mysteries focus on the public life of Jesus — the heart of the Gospels. They round out the Rosary as a prayerful meditation of the complete salvation story.

Each of the Joyful, Luminous, Sorrowful, and Glorious mysteries is rooted in Scripture. Meditating — even briefly — on each mystery enriches prayer. It also creates a meditative space for listening to God. After you have prayed the Sign of the Cross, the Apostles' Creed, and the Glory Be, which begin every Rosary, determine which mysteries should be prayed for the day. (See the weekly mystery schedule on page 143.) Proceed by praying the five decades of the Rosary with the mysteries suggested for that day.

(In fact, you can pray the mysteries that seem most appropriate for the day, your circumstances, needs, or concerns. The days that are set aside for praying the four sets of mysteries are suggested times so that those praying with the Rosary can reflect on the full Gospel story.)

Before you begin each decade, read or say the mystery title. This is the time to reflect on the meaning of this mystery. Recall or reread the Scripture passage provided in this book for the mystery. Picture the event in your mind. Bring to mind, as well, what you read in *Praying the Rosary for Intercession* about this mystery.

Finally, read the mystery prayer and reflect on the suggestions for intercession given for this mystery. Plan to intercede, as well, for your own intentions or those you've been asked to remember in your prayers.

PRAYING THE ROSARY

From the Crucifix to the Rosary Medallion

Pray the Sign of the Cross, the Apostles' Creed, the Our Father, three Hail Marys and the Glory Be. These prayers begin every Rosary, regardless of the mysteries, in the following order:

- Sign of the Cross
- Apostles' Creed
- Our Father
- Hail Mary (three)
- Glory Be

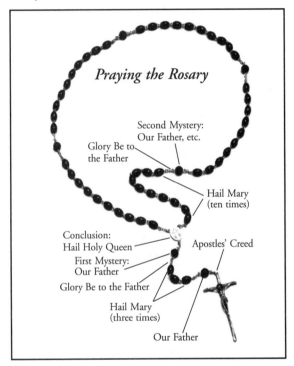

Praying the Rosary

Second Mystery:
Our Father, etc.

Glory Be to
the Father

Hail Mary
(ten times)

Conclusion:
Hail Holy Queen

Apostles' Creed

First Mystery:
Our Father

Glory Be to the Father

Hail Mary
(three times)

Our Father

Praying Five Decades (*Joyful, Luminous, Sorrowful, Glorious*) *of the Rosary*

Meditate with the mystery prayers and intentions listed below. Then pray each decade of the Rosary as follows:

- Our Father
- Hail Mary (ten)
- Glory Be

Consider praying the Fátima Prayer following each decade (that is, after the Glory Be and before the next mystery).

Concluding Prayers

After you have prayed all five decades, you can conclude with the Hail Holy Queen or any other Marian prayer. These prayers are optional and are not part of the established Rosary prayers.

MYSTERY PRAYERS AND INTENTIONS

—————————— *The Joyful Mysteries* ——————————

1. The Annunciation

Prayer

God, you chose to invite Mary, a teenage girl in Nazareth, to be the sinless mother of your son, Jesus. Your shining angel Gabriel appeared to her announcing your request. Every day, you send invitations to me, as well. Mary, the Mother of Jesus, please help me to see the Father's invitations in my life. Ask God to strengthen me so that I may joyfully say yes to him, just as you did. Amen.

Intentions

- Humility and openness to God's will in our lives.
- Respect and reverence for the unborn child.
- The conception and birth of healthy children for couples who want to be parents.
- Your own intention(s).

2. The Visitation

Prayer

God, our Creator, you fashioned the loving heart of Mary, who became the mother of Jesus. In her joy over this great blessing, she traveled to see and assist her cousin Elizabeth. Mary gave the loving gift of her presence, her care, and her desire to help when help was needed. Mary, help me to lovingly share my presence and my help wherever I go. Amen.

Intentions

- Visiting and personal outreach to others.
- Ministry to pregnant mothers.
- Offering companionship, the gift of presence.
- Your own intention(s).

3. The Birth of Our Lord

Prayer

Father of the Redeemer, your angels filled the Bethlehem sky with rejoicing on the night your son, Jesus, was born. You gave the world the gift you had always promised. The Son of God was born among us. He came to live with us, to die for us, and to save us. Mary, you and Joseph welcomed the newborn Jesus with so much love. Help me to welcome Jesus into my heart and into my life each day. Amen.

Intentions

- Welcoming and caring for each child born.
- Protection and respect for children's rights.
- Support for families.
- Your own intention(s).

4. The Presentation in the Temple

Prayer

Loving God, Mary and Joseph honored you and Jewish law. They presented Jesus at the Temple forty days after his birth, even though he was already consecrated to you. Their hearts were humble, faithful, and obedient. Mary, because you and Joseph were faithful, God answered the prayers of Simeon and Anna to see the Messiah. Help me to be faithful and strong, honoring what's expected of me, as I grapple with the demands of life. Amen.

Intentions
- Dedication of our children to God.
- Honoring religious customs and laws.
- Faithfulness in responsibilities.
- Your own intention(s).

5. The Finding of Jesus in the Temple

Prayer

Almighty Father, your son, Jesus, was already growing "in wisdom and age and favor" when Mary and Joseph finally found him in the Temple. They had been searching for him, and their hearts were full of fear. Jesus said that he needed to be in his "Father's house." Mary, you knew that your son was growing up and that he was beginning to accept his mission. Help me to "let go and let God" work in my life and in those I love. Amen.

Intentions
- Missing children and young people.
- The grace to "let go and let God. . . ."
- Honor and obedience for parents.
- Your own intention(s).

—————————— The Luminous Mysteries ——————————

1. The Baptism in the Jordan

Prayer

Almighty God, Jesus, your "beloved Son," was baptized in the Jordan, just like the thousands of others coming from all over Israel and Judea. Your Holy Spirit filled Jesus in a new way, equipping him for the public life that was beginning. Mary, you knew that Jesus was following his call and beginning the work for which he had been born. Help me to see and embrace my own vocation, and to welcome the special work God gives to me. Amen.

Intentions
- The baptized and those seeking new life through Baptism.
- Renewal through the Holy Spirit.
- Those seeking a vocation.
- Your own intention(s).

2. The Wedding Feast of Cana

Prayer

Loving Creator, it was you who created man and woman in your own image. You gave them to each other in the garden and saw that it was good. You are the author of marriage and family, and their joys and blessings. Mary, you asked Jesus to work his first miracle for newlyweds in Cana. Jesus graciously complied. Help me to ask God to strengthen and bless all married couples and their families. Amen.

Intentions
- Married couples and those planning to be married.
- For love and joy in relationships.
- Devotion to Mary as an advocate.
- Your own intention(s).

3. The Proclamation of the Kingdom of God

Prayer

Heavenly Father, you sent Jesus into the world with such Good News! He announced that your Kingdom was being established among us. It meant glad tidings to the poor, liberty to captives, and recovery of sight to the blind.

Mary, you must have been so happy that your son's Kingdom work was beginning. Show me where I can help in this Kingdom work — sharing glad tidings and bringing liberty to captives. Amen.

Intentions

- Acceptance of the Good News of Jesus Christ.
- New evangelization for the world.
- All clergy and ministers of the Word.
- Your own intention(s).

4. The Transfiguration

Prayer

Almighty God, you showed the magnificent and shining glory of your divine Son, Jesus, to Peter, James, and John. Jesus was transfigured before their eyes. Those three apostles saw him, as he truly is — the Son of God. Their faith was strengthened, and their hearts were moved. Mary, you didn't need to see your son shining with light to know who he was. On the days when my faith needs support, help me remember that he is my God. He shines with a blinding and unforgettable light. Amen.

Intentions

- Recognition that Jesus is God.
- Seeing God's hidden glory in creation.
- Those in need of personal transformation.
- Your own intention(s).

5. The Institution of the Eucharist

Prayer

God, your son, Jesus, deeply loved his brothers and sisters and wanted to remain with them until the end of time. So, he gave them his Body and Blood under the appearance of bread and wine. He remained with his first disciples, and he remains with us in the Eucharist. Mary, you understood the boundless love of your son. Remind me to cherish the Eucharist. Don't let me take this "bread of life" for granted. Amen.

Intentions

· Love of Jesus in the Eucharist.
· A growing commitment to feed the hungry.
· "Food" for those with spiritual hungers.
· Your own intention(s).

——————— *The Sorrowful Mysteries* ———————

1. The Agony in the Garden

Prayer

Merciful God, Jesus, your Son, was beginning the agonizing journey to his cruel and painful death. He knew that all along the way, there would be terrifying pain. Jesus asked to be spared from a horrible death on the cross, but he also promised to do your will. Mary, surely you knew that the suffering of Jesus was beginning. Strengthen me in times of anxiety, stress, fear, and loneliness. Help me to do God's will, even when it hurts to do so. Amen.

Intentions

· Those suffering mental and emotional stress.
· People who feel abandoned or lonely.
· Courage and faith in the midst of great suffering.
· Your own intention(s).

2. The Scourging at the Pillar

Prayer

God, Our Father, Jesus was so cruelly beaten and abused. So much pain was inflicted upon him. He struggled bravely to stand and take it. Roman soldiers merely carried out what the people of Jerusalem had asked for — the vicious and cruel scourging of an innocent man headed for the cross. Mary, every blow Jesus received must have wounded your poor heart. Support and fortify me when unavoidable suffering and pain come my way. Show me how to help and pray for others who are suffering. Amen.

Intentions

- People suffering physical pain.
- An end to physical violence and torture.
- Compassion and justice for prisoners.
- Your own intention(s).

3. The Crowning with Thorns

Prayer

Holy God, you saw your divine Son mocked and spat upon. The Kingdom of God that he announced became the subject of a cruel and hideous joke. Jesus, your suffering servant, was taunted and tortured with a painful crown of thorns. Mary, somehow, you felt the pain and humiliation that Jesus was enduring. Your heart was breaking for him. When I am humiliated and diminished, remind me to suffer without bitterness, without the desire for revenge. Let me act and speak in a way that honors the dignity of every person. Amen.

Intentions

- Those suffering emotional abuse and ridicule.
- Personal patience, humility, and courage.
- Conversion of those who abuse and persecute others.
- Your own intention(s).

4. The Carrying of the Cross

Prayer

God, your beloved Son was forced to carry the cross-beam on which he would be nailed. Jesus was "like a lamb led to slaughter / or a sheep silent before shearers, / he did not open his mouth" (Isaiah 53:7). Mary, another sword of grief pierced your heart when you saw your beautiful and loving son stumbling on his "Way of the Cross." Pray for me when I am asked to shoulder a cross and make my way to suffering, and maybe to death. Amen.

Intentions

- Growing love of Jesus, our Redeemer.
- Strength to carry God-given crosses.
- Help for those who are burdened.
- Your own intention(s).

5. The Crucifixion

Prayer

Father, finally your Son didn't have the strength to take another breath. He surrendered his spirit to you, and died. The bruised and bloody body of Jesus testified to the greatest sacrifice imaginable. Your sinless Son, our Savior, was executed like a common criminal. Mary, when you witnessed your son's death, you must have wished for your own. Yet, you bowed to the Father's will. Strengthen me when I am on the way to God. "Pray for us sinners, now and at the hour of our death." Amen.

Intentions

- An end to capital punishment.
- A blessed, peaceful death for the dying.
- Conversion of those supporting or considering euthanasia.
- Your own intention(s).

———————— *The Glorious Mysteries* ————————

1. The Resurrection

Prayer

Glorious God, your Son, Jesus, conquered death and rose on the third day. The grave could not hold him. Through his sufferings and death, Jesus had redeemed all of your children for all time. Mary, when Jesus rose from the dead, your heart was filled with Resurrection joy. Teach me to see beyond my sufferings and coming death. Help me to renew and share my Resurrection faith each day. Amen.

Intentions

- New faith in the Resurrection.
- Renewed joy in Christian churches.
- Care for the endangered environment and the Earth.
- Your own intention(s).

2. The Ascension

Prayer

Father of us all, after Jesus rose and spent forty precious days with his followers, he ascended to you. As the Son of God, he took his place at your right hand. One day, he will return to judge the living and the dead. Mary, Mother of our Redeemer, you heard Jesus remind his followers, "You will be my witnesses to the ends of the earth." Help me to see how Jesus wants me to witness in his name, today. Amen.

Intentions

- Mentors and those they mentor.
- Courage and faith when transitions come.
- Accepting Jesus as a teacher and guide.
- Your own intention(s).

3. The Descent of the Holy Spirit

Prayer

Holy Spirit, you came with a rush of wind and fire upon the disciples of Jesus in Jerusalem. You filled them with wonderful gifts and charisms to continue the Kingdom work of Jesus. Mary, you, too, knew the mighty but sweet power of the Spirit. Open my eyes and heart to recognize and use the gifts I have. They come from the Holy Spirit. I am part of Pentecost. Amen.

Intentions

- Faith in the Holy Spirit.
- Renewal and new fire in the Church.
- Using our gifts to build the Kingdom of God.
- Your own intention(s).

4. The Assumption

Prayer

Creator God, when you created the mother of your Son in her mother's womb, you set her free from the stain of sin. Immaculately conceived, she said yes to the plan you had for her and the sinful world. After the end of her earthly life, Jesus called her to heaven, body and soul, so that corruption would never touch her. Mary, I rejoice in your assumption. Remind me each day, that I — and all the children of God — can have that same destiny. Amen.

Intentions

- Those afraid of death.
- Honor for Mary as the Mother of God's Son.
- Faith in the resurrection of the body.
- Your own intention(s).

5. The Coronation of Our Lady Queen of Heaven

Prayer

Almighty God, you knew that Mary was beyond compare among your creatures. We agree and give her countless titles. She is "Seat of wisdom," "Mirror of justice," "Mystical rose," "House of gold," "Morning star," "Gate of heaven," "Ark of the covenant," and much, much more. In heaven, you made her Queen. Mary, here on earth, you are also our gentle, loving queen. Today, as I go about my day, please guide me. Show me how to serve the Kingdom of God here on earth. Amen.

Intentions

- Understanding of Mary's role in salvation.
- Support for rightful authority.
- Honor for Mary in all Christian churches.
- Your own intention(s).

ROSARY PRAYERS

Sign of the Cross

In the name of the Father, and of the Son, and of the Holy Spirit. Amen.

Apostles' Creed

I believe in God,
the Father almighty,
Creator of heaven and earth,
and in Jesus Christ, his only Son, our Lord,
who was conceived by the Holy Spirit,
born of the Virgin Mary,
suffered under Pontius Pilate,
was crucified, died and was buried;
he descended into hell;
on the third day he rose again from the dead;

he ascended into heaven,
and is seated at the right hand
    of God the Father almighty;
from there he will come to judge
    the living and the dead.
I believe in the Holy Spirit,
the holy catholic Church,
the communion of saints,
the forgiveness of sins,
the resurrection of the body,
and life everlasting. Amen.

Our Father

Our Father, who art in heaven, hallowed be thy name. Thy kingdom come; thy will be done on earth as it is in heaven. Give us this day our daily bread; and forgive us our trespasses as we forgive those who trespass against us; and lead us not into temptation, but deliver us from evil. Amen.

Hail Mary

Hail, Mary, full of grace, the Lord is with thee; blessed art thou among women, and blessed is the fruit of thy womb, Jesus. Holy Mary, Mother of God, pray for us sinners, now and at the hour of our death. Amen.

Glory Be

Glory be to the Father, and to the Son, and to the Holy Spirit. As it was in the beginning, is now, and ever shall be, world without end. Amen.

Fátima Prayer

O my Jesus, forgive us our sins, save us from the fires of hell, lead all souls to heaven, especially those in most need of your mercy.

Hail Holy Queen

Hail, holy Queen, Mother of Mercy, our life, our sweetness and our hope. To thee do we cry, poor banished children of Eve; to thee do we send up our sighs, mourning, and weeping in this valley of tears. Turn then, most gracious advocate, thine eyes of mercy toward us, and after this, our exile, show unto us the blessed fruit of thy womb, Jesus. O clement, O loving, O Sweet Virgin Mary.

V. Pray for us, O holy Mother of God.
R. That we may be made worthy of the promises of Christ.

Concluding Rosary Prayer

Let us pray: O God, whose only begotten Son, by his life, death, and resurrection, has purchased for us the rewards of eternal life, grant, we beseech thee, that meditating upon these mysteries of the Most Holy Rosary of the Blessed Virgin Mary, we may imitate what they contain and obtain what they promise, through the same Christ our Lord. Amen.

ABOUT THE AUTHOR

CATHERINE M. ODELL is a freelance journalist, editor, and author of twelve books, including Our Sunday Visitor's *Those Who Saw Her, Faustina: Apostle of Divine Mercy,* and *Solanus Casey: The Story of Father Solanus.*